Creating Culturally Responsive Schools

Creating Culturally Responsive Schools

One Classroom at a Time

Michele M. Wages, PhD

ROWMAN & LITTLEFIELD
Lanham • Boulder • New York • London

Published by Rowman & Littlefield
A wholly owned subsidiary of The Rowman & Littlefield Publishing Group, Inc.
4501 Forbes Boulevard, Suite 200, Lanham, Maryland 20706
www.rowman.com

Unit A, Whitacre Mews, 26-34 Stannary Street, London SE11 4AB

Copyright © 2015 by Michele M. Wages

All rights reserved. No part of this book may be reproduced in any form or by any electronic or mechanical means, including information storage and retrieval systems, without written permission from the publisher, except by a reviewer who may quote passages in a review.

British Library Cataloguing in Publication Information Available

Library of Congress Cataloging-in-Publication Data

Wages, Michele, 1965-
Creating culturally responsive schools : one classroom at a time / Michele Wages.
pages cm
Includes bibliographical references.
ISBN 978-1-4758-1808-6 (cloth : alk. paper) -- ISBN 978-1-4758-1809-3 (pbk.) -- ISBN 978-1-4758-1810-9 (electronic)
1. Multicultural education--United States. 2. Cultural awareness--United States. 3. Teaching--Social aspects--United States. 4. Teacher-student relationships--United States. I. Title.
LC1099.3.W34 2015
370.1170973--dc23
2015014094

∞ ™ The paper used in this publication meets the minimum requirements of American National Standard for Information Sciences Permanence of Paper for Printed Library Materials, ANSI/NISO Z39.48-1992.

Printed in the United States of America

Contents

Foreword	vii
Preface	ix
Introduction	xiii
Background	xv
1 Preparing the Teacher	1
2 Supporting the Teacher	17
3 Learning Within the Context of Culture	29
4 Managing the Classroom with Cultural Responsiveness	49
5 Reshaping the Curriculum	63
6 Culturally Responsive Lessons, Lesson Plans, and Assessment	87
Conclusion	107
Appendix A	109
Glossary	115
References	117

About the Author 127

Foreword

In this groundbreaking text Michele Wages makes the case, clearly and forcefully, that culturally responsive pedagogy in which students' unique cultural strengths are nurtured is needed to increase student achievement—for all students—not only those who are considered English Language Learners. Because the cultural assimilation in today's classrooms is growing exponentially, teachers no longer have a choice as to whether they want to interact with or wish to ignore diversity. Wages argues convincingly that it is urgent that educators become culturally capable and knowledgeable. By studying the cultural backgrounds of all their students, she informs us that teachers can avoid some of the behavior and learning problems that are seemingly on the rise in today's classrooms.

Helping teachers shape culturally responsive classrooms is why this book was created. From the opening pages, Dr. Wages makes a rock-solid argument that understanding the explicit knowledge required by teachers about cultural diversity is imperative in all subject areas. According to Dr. Wages' research, given today's increase in the number of diverse classrooms, it is essential that learning more about the ingrained values and beliefs of students in order to meet their needs is no longer an option. It is an urgent priority.

This text provides the reader with a clear, lucid description of the characteristics of what a culturally responsive classroom looks like, how a culturally responsive teacher meets the diverse cultural needs of students, and offers a workable framework to implement the required changes. To do such, the text tackles the tough issues head on from preparing and supporting teachers, to addressing and managing the culturally responsive classroom, to providing the classroom practitioner with the support needed to make over their classrooms with effective instructional strategies. Implementing the ideas and principles presented in this text will help teachers and administrators to know how to reshape the curriculum to be more culturally responsible and create culturally responsive lessons, lesson plans, and assessments. This is an outstanding and readable book that takes readers on a learning journey. If you have longed for practical suggestions that lead to very productive culturally appropriate classrooms, this is your book!

—Dr. Mario Campanaro
Author of *Teaching Figure 19: The Instructional Strategies That Matter Most* and *Developing Strategic Readers: Lesson Plans for Teaching Figure 19 to Harness the Power of the Cognitive Strategies*

Preface

The numbers of culturally and linguistically diverse students in our public schools has been increasing steadily for years. Even with this knowledge, college teacher education programs are not successfully preparing future teachers to have the culturally responsive education pedagogy needed in today's classrooms (Gay, 2002).

This creates a teacher workforce that is ill-prepared for the classrooms they have been assigned and unfairly held accountable for the student achievement in them. According to Marilyn Cochran-Smith (2004), resistance to educational changes usually occurs from the teacher's fear of addressing issues such as race or racism in the classroom. Today's schools require teachers to not only know what they are teaching but who they are teaching and how to do it (Kea & Utley, 1988).

Explicit knowledge about cultural diversity is imperative. Within this knowledge base, an understanding of cultural characteristics and contributions of different ethnic groups is essential. The needed knowledge goes beyond awareness of different ethnic groups and must recognize that different values and beliefs exist. Educators need detailed factual information about the particulars of different ethnic groups' culture. "Having this in-depth knowledge will help the teacher to make schooling more interesting and stimulating to their ethnically diverse students. Often it is thought that specific subjects such as math and science are incompatible with cultural diversity. Geneva Gay (2002) believes that we must realize that there is a place for cultural diversity in every subject taught in school."

Quality research-based pedagogy must be used that is responsive to learning emotional and social needs of ethnically and linguistically diverse students and is necessary of today's educators. Diversity is defined as individual differences (personality, learning styles, and life experience) and group/social differences (race, ethnicity, gender, sexual orientation, country of origin, and ability) that can be engaged in the service of learning.

Success in today's diverse classrooms is reliant on the use of culturally responsive teaching. Geneva Gay (2000) defines culturally responsive teaching as using the cultural knowledge, prior experiences, and performance styles of diverse students to make learning more appropriate and effective for them; it teaches to and through the strengths of these students.

Helping teachers shape culturally responsive classrooms is why this book was created. Given the increase in diversity in today's schools and classrooms, learning more about students in order to meet their needs is an urgent priority.

This book will walk the reader through the characteristics of a culturally responsive teacher in chapter 1 and move to supporting the teacher in chapter 2. The third and fourth chapters address learning within the context of culture and managing the culturally responsive classroom. The last two chapters then provide strategies in how to reshape the curriculum to be more culturally responsible and create culturally responsive lessons, lesson plans, and assessments.

As in any educational resource, take what you like and leave the rest. It is my hope as a lifelong educator that some of this information will make your life easier, better clarify misconceptions, and provide you with real-life examples to better address the diversity you face in today's classrooms.

Introduction

A powerful statement describing the overpowering influence the teacher has on the classroom was made by Haim Ginott in 1995 when he said:

> I have come to a frightening conclusion, I am the decisive element in the classroom. It is my personal approach that creates the climate. It is my daily mood that makes the weather. As a teacher, I possess tremendous power to make a child's life miserable or joyous. I can be a tool of torture or an instrument of inspiration. I can humiliate or humor, hurt or heal. In all situations, it is my response that decides whether a crisis will be escalated or de-escalated, and a child humanized or dehumanized. (p. 302)

With so much cultural mixing in today's classrooms, teachers no longer have a choice as to whether they want to interact with diversity or not. It is imperative that educators become culturally competent. By studying the cultural backgrounds of their students, teachers can learn to avoid some of the problems that surface each day in the public school classroom.

Today's classrooms are extremely diverse and many educators are not prepared for the increasing need for culturally responsive teaching. Within the pages of this book you will discover not only what it means to be a culturally responsive educator, but also how to strengthen a schools' staff in cultural awareness, respect, and value, and how to use this knowledge to increase all student achievement. Each chapter is self-sufficient, allowing the reader to utilize only those parts of the book needed. This is an invaluable educator resource addressing current classroom demographics.

—Dr. Michele M. Wages

Background

Geneva Gay (2000) also states "culture is central to learning." It plays a role not only in communicating and receiving information, but also in shaping the thinking process of groups and individuals. A pedagogy that acknowledges, responds to, and celebrates fundamental cultures offers full, equitable access to education for students from all cultures.

A focus on the student-centered approach is key to the culturally responsive pedagogy in which students' unique cultural strengths are nurtured to create an increase in student achievement. Little (1999) adds that three specific areas must be reformed in order to make the institution more culturally responsive. These areas are:

1. Organization of school
2. School policy and procedures
3. Community involvement

According to Lynch (2011), there are three functional dimensions in culturally responsive pedagogy:

1. Institutional: This dimension emphasizes the need for reform in the organization of schools, in school policies and procedures, and in community involvement with regard to cultural factors. The institutional dimension reflects the administration and its policies and values. The educational system is the institution that provides the physical and political structure for the school. Paul Gorski and Bob Covert (2000) state that six conditions must be implemented in classrooms to ensure culturally educational curriculum and setting support for students.

    a. Teachers must ensure that every student has an equal opportunity to achieve her or his full potential.
    b. Students must be geared up to competently involve themselves in a more progressive intercultural society.
    c. Teachers must be geared up to effectively facilitate learning for every student no matter how culturally different from or similar to him- or herself.
    d. The school must be a dynamic participant in ending subjugation within their own territory, to produce a socially and critically active awareness in students.
    e. Student-centered and comprehensive, the voices and experiences of the students should be implied in their education.
    f. Educators, activists, and others must take a more active role in reexamining all educational practices and how they affect the learning of all students: testing methods; teaching approaches; evaluation and assessment; school.

2. Personal: This dimension consists of two components due to the need for teachers to honestly examine their attitudes, beliefs, values, and their long-term goals in order to create a more welcoming and safe environment for the students and families (Villegas & Lucas, 2002). This clarification in understanding allows the teachers to better appreciate differences and provide unbiased instruction that addresses the needs of all their students. Relationships with students are directly impacted by teachers' values and thus, teachers must adjust their negative feelings toward any culture, language, or ethnic group. The fear that their personal values might reflect prejudices or project racism toward certain groups is often the reason teachers are resistant to cultural responsiveness. Once biases are identified and better understood, teachers are able to create an atmosphere of trust and acceptance for their students which results in increasing student success.

3. Instructional: Refers to "practice and challenges associated with implementing cultural responsiveness in the classroom. When tools of instruction (books, teaching methods, and activities) are incompatible with, or worse, marginalize the students' cultural experiences, a disconnect with school is likely" (Irvine, 1990). This rejection of school for some students can materialize in the form of simply underachieving, but for others it could cause the child to not perform at all, or worse, drop out of school completely. The culturally responsive model shows teachers how to recognize and utilize the students' culture and language in their instruction which magnifies respect for the students' personal and community identities.

Chapter One

Preparing the Teacher

"A people without the knowledge of their past history, origin and culture is like a tree without roots."
—Marcus Garvey

According to Hackett (2003), developing a strong cultural identity should be the focus for educators who are responsible for teaching values, skills, and knowledge to the whole child so they can not only have success in school but also be a positive impact in society by linking classroom teaching to out-of-school personal experiences and community situations (p. 329).

Even without English Language Learner (ELL) classrooms, every school in the United States today contains students of different socioeconomic backgrounds, family structures, and religious beliefs. Each student also comes with a family cultural history, individual personality, and varied interests and abilities. Today's teachers need to consider these variables in cultural values when creating lessons to ensure they are not meaningless or confusing to students.

For many teachers, regardless of experience, thinking about race and culture presents a new experience that has not been confronted before. Howard (2003) calls this the luxury of ignorance. White teachers especially may define the acknowledgment of racial and cultural differences as counter-productive and can often exhibit what has become known as the colorblind approach to teaching. Most white teachers have never visualized themselves in terms of racial beings, unlike their black and brown students. This presents an issue in that there is a lack of understanding as to how central one's race is to their identity. This refusal to acknowledge this component of their students' backgrounds intensifies the teacher's implementation of colorblind ideologies which results in them ignoring or undervaluing the children in their classroom.

INTRINSICALLY MOTIVATING STUDENTS

When a student is engaged in learning, it is the visible outcome of motivation. Their energy is directed in the pursuit of a goal. As human beings, our motivation is influenced by our emotions. In addition, our emotions are also socialized through culture. As a result, our emotions are energized by our culture, the deeply learned confluence of language, beliefs, values, and behaviors that pervades every aspect of our lives. As teachers, we must understand that a student's response to a learning activity reflects their culture. Instead of knowing what to do to students, educators must work with students to better understand their knowledge and enthusiasm for learning. Using this as a focal point, when a teacher uses motivation effectively, they are modeling culturally responsive teaching.

Human nature programs us to be curious, to be active, to make meaning from everyday experiences, and to value certain things. No matter one's culture, motivation resides inside us. The connection students make when they realize what they are learning makes sense causes intrinsic motivation. Teachers influence this motivation through knowing their perspectives, understanding who they are naturally and culturally, and by acknowledging all as unique and active. Too often however, teachers battle an extrinsically dominated educational system where grades and class rank are emphasized, making it difficult to apply intrinsic motivation theories. Unfortunately, when extrinsic rewards continue to be primary motivators, intrinsic motivation is dampened.

Cultural competence is the ability to interact effectively with people of different cultures. It comprises four components:

- Awareness of one's cultural views
- Attitudes toward cultural differences
- Knowledge of different cultural practices and world views
- Cross-cultural skills

Ladson-Billings (1994) states that the pedagogy of culturally responsible teaching recognizes the importance of including students' cultural experiences and beliefs in all aspects of learning. A starting point for teachers toward intrinsic motivation is to be respectful of different cultures when creating a classroom culture that all students can accept.

Wlodkowski and Ginsberg (1995) developed a motivational framework for teachers to assist in increasing intrinsic motivation. The framework consists of four elements:

1. Establish Inclusion: This element emphasizes the human purpose of what is being learned and its relationship to the students' experiences. This creates a hopeful view of people and their capacity to change and shares ownership in pointing out behaviors or practices that discriminate in the classroom. It includes collaborative learning approaches, such as writing

groups and peer teaching, and must be structured around ground rules, learning communities, and cooperative base groups.

2. Develop Positive Attitude: Through personal relevance and choice, a favorable disposition and positive attitude is created. This element relates teaching and learning activities to students' experiences or previous knowledge and encourages them to make choices based on these experiences and values. This may include setting clear learning goals and problem-solving goals, learning contracts and approaches based on multiple intelligences, and can include teacher/student/parent conferences.

3. Enhance Meaning: Developing learning experiences that are challenging and thoughtful to enhance meaning by including the student's perspectives and values. The challenging learning experiences based on real-life issues encourage discussion of relevant experiences and incorporate student perspectives into classroom dialogue.

4. Engender Competence: Students learning what they value creates an understanding that engenders competence. Materials should include multiple ways to represent knowledge and skills and allow for attainment of outcomes at different points in time, thus encouraging self-assessment in the forms of portfolios and process-folios.

When a teacher creates an intrinsically motivated environment, engagement in learning increases. This motivational framework provides a holistic and culturally responsive way to create, plan, and refine teaching activities, lessons, and assessment measures.

PEDAGOGY OF CULTURALLY RESPONSIVE TEACHING

A culturally responsive pedagogy opens up channels for the discussion of difficult topics—like racism, discrimination, and prejudice—and provides students opportunities to engage in meaningful discussion that deepens learning. Because this pedagogy acknowledges the presence of racism that creates distorted and negative images of the cultures, histories, and possibilities of people of color (Beauboeuf-Lafontant, 1999), culturally responsive classrooms can develop a space where harmful images can be deconstructed and positive self and cultural affirmations displayed.

Hanley and Noblit (2009) state that culturally responsive pedagogy consists of a set of concepts (culturally relevant, congruent, and appropriate) made of subtle distinctions. Culture is often referred to in research as the ways of being, doing, and sense making. Culture is one tool humans use during activity to produce new ways of being, doing, and sense making across generations and social contexts

Many cultures exist in the United States. The dominant culture is that of the White Anglo ethnicity in which many cultures are subject to its dominance. For example, the African American culture emerges from both Africa and America's history and is considered communal, spiritual, resilient, and humanistic. This culture also incorporates verbal expressiveness, personal style, emotional vitality, and musicality and has an emphasis on facing life without pretense (Hanley & Noblit, 2009). Today's American economic and political conditions are dominated by European cultural norms centering on individualism, competition, and emotional restraint.

A culturally responsive pedagogy consists of using the cultural attributes during the development of curriculum, instructional processes, classroom organization, motivational strategies, classroom management, and assessment. Creating a culturally responsive pedagogy uses all these means to engage student interest as well as develop ownership of learning and inspire achievement. For the purposes of this book, getting students to think critically about racial socialization and identity, including the acknowledgment of racism and racial oppression as they achieve academic and other successes is the basis for content and pedagogical means. Resilience refers to the remarkable ability of humans to recover from adversity, and resiliency is a highly desirable state for children and youth in the direst of circumstances (Hanley & Noblit, 2009). The aim for culturally relevant pedagogy is to ensure that educators acknowledge and honor the diverse viewpoints of their student population. To accomplish this, they must also refrain from promoting homogeneous perspectives as universal beliefs. Dingus (2003) states no student should have to sacrifice cultural heritage, ethnic identity and social networks in order to obtain an education (p. 99).

Unfortunately, the majority of schools in America determine academic success as a multifaceted concept that focuses on grades, achievement test scores, and on learning the key concepts and strategies of a planned program of study. It is very apparent that the system is failing in growing culturally literate and tolerant young adults.

THEMES FOR CULTURALLY RESPONSIVE PEDAGOGY

Culturally responsive pedagogy needs to be designed so that the teacher promotes racial identity, resilience, and achievement. Here are some examples of themes based on research from Hanley & Noblit (2009) as to how this can be accomplished:

1. Involve the community: Active participation of the community is a necessity for the success of a culturally responsive pedagogy or program. Culture is always changing and varies even within a racial group, community, or among family members and is a valuable resource for educators about the needs and resources of the children in their classrooms. The challenge for today's educators is effectively designing a program or pedagogy for a culture that they are unfamiliar with or that is not their own. Increasing their skills in inquiry and listening to both their students and students' families is the first step.
2. Use culture to promote racial identity: Adaptations in instructional practice, classroom organization and management, and increasing motivation is required for an effective culturally responsive pedagogy. The rule of thumb for most education programs is to involve key characteristics of the home culture and focus on the development of strategies in how to best use culture in the creation of a positive racial identity that promotes resilience and success in all social institutions.
3. Use culture and racial identity as an asset: An asset to the learning and development within a culturally responsive program is race. A student's culture should be viewed as a strength to be built upon for optimal learning to occur. Programs need to be affirmative of the student and their culture and not set a stigmatizing tone. Ensuring that racial stereotypes will not be used against the student develops trust and helps strengthen the culturally responsive program.
4. Educate about racism and racial uplift: Providing accurate information about racial oppression and racism to promote

awareness will increase achievement and resilience in the face of racial oppression.
5. Develop caring relationships: Developing caring relationships with a cultural focus needs to be handled with caution. The teacher needs to remember that the student will interpret what is caring from their culture, not from the culture of the person offering a caring relationship.
6. Assume success: Addressing or identifying problems and deficiencies, for the most part, is the primary focus of most programs. Far too often this causes the program's success to have severe obstacles. Programs should be implemented with the mindset that the wealth of culture and experience each student brings should be used to build academic, cultural, and racial strengths.
7. Promote active learning, problem-based instruction, and student involvement: Adaptations in instructional practice, classroom management, and student engagement are needed for the culturally responsive pedagogy. High expectations should be supported by educators, parents, and students to be involved through the use of decision making, critical thinking, and respect for differences in their active learning and problem-based instruction so it can be applied to real-world situations.
8. Employ the arts: Cultural productions within the arts are ideal vehicles for culturally responsive programming. Engaging students' cultural and racial identities has shown that learning happens in a wide range of competencies.
9. Acknowledge the challenges: A change in educators' frames of reference about culture of children and families is needed for effective culturally responsive pedagogy. Teacher training

and support needs to be in place to help unravel many educational views of culture's place in today's classrooms. Progress in the creation and offering of educational programs for teachers is in the near future. This change will be challenging and difficult and will require courage and tenacity but will be so rewarding for everyone in the end.

Another key element is in preparing the teacher to work with culturally diverse students and their families. Teachers must come to understand the real-life experiences that the students they teach and their families come with. Creating plausible situations which allow families a legitimate voice in the curriculum is a key element. This voice can provide advice to teachers on how to balance high stakes accountability testing with survival skills children need to thrive at school. Some suggestions include:

1. Call each child's family with positive information, not just negative
2. With today's technology, emailing each student's family with positive information is a doable option
3. Video media can also be used to capture a student in action allowing the parent to see the student's successes

Developing positive interactions with families and encouraging family involvement allows families to feel more in sync with the school climate and culture. This is also a great way for parents to feel welcome in including their perspectives in planning and implementation of professional development opportunities, school activities, and community events.

Ethnicity, race, and culture are substantial parts of a student's identity. Once educators recognize this, children can be respected and represented in the classroom community and the teacher can move from colorblindness to cultural responsiveness. Regardless if the gap is due to racial, ethnic, or cultural differences between students and teachers, it can result in a misunderstanding of student behavior, academic ability, and teacher expectations (Irvine, 2003). It is important to remember that simply because a teacher is the same race or culture as her students does not mean she or he is automatically culturally responsive (Nieto, 1999).

COMMUNICATING HIGH EXPECTATIONS TO STUDENTS

Students' performance is highly affected by teachers' expectations. Realistic and high expectations are not only held high for the teachers themselves, but also for all students. This expectation is reflected in the classroom climate created and the positive perception of their students' ability to succeed. Classrooms where students are expected to be hardworking, interested, and successful produce students who are. This has been supported by the research which finds that "students who feel they have supportive, caring teachers are more motivated to engage in academic work than students with unsupportive, uncaring teachers" (McCombs, 2001).

Effective teachers use their actions and words to communicate their expectations and attitudes. These perceived expectations also can affect the students' motivation and self-concept. Sometimes teachers, either purposefully or unknowingly, show favoritism to high achievers by interacting with them more frequently, giving them more time to answer questions, and increasing the amount of positive feedback given to them. Unfortunately, the opposite happens for low achieving students where often times they are seated in the back of the room resulting in fewer opportunities to respond to questions. These students also receive more criticism for incorrect responses and are given little or no wait time to answer questions before the teacher provides the answer or moves on.

This creates frustration for students that are not supported to meet the teachers' expectations. To avoid this, guards in setting too low or too high expectations need to be in place especially for students with special needs and for gifted students. In order to increase the drive for students to achieve, the students need to first believe that achievement is possible. This means multiple opportunities for success need to occur for all students.

Achieving goals and focusing on long-term improvement can be difficult in a system that focuses on grades and test mastery. Effective teachers strive to help students set goals that are achievable while also teaching them how to evaluate, critique, and analyze their work in order to identify strengths and address weaknesses.

When teachers set high expectations and hold students accountable, their academic performance and self-esteem are greatly enhanced.

The most important thing to remember is that effective teachers treat all students the same. Culture, socioeconomic status, or special needs are not perceived as barriers to students' ability to succeed, but confidence in all capabilities are expressed. Creating this positive self-fulfilling energy causes students to produce, behave, and achieve in accordance with the teacher's expectations.

The fact that students perceive teachers' actions as a mirror of themselves may result in a need for teachers to use caution. Teachers cannot simply verbalize that they believe in students' abilities and not support or act on it. Realistic expectations need to be set for all students when giving presentations, holding discussions, making assignments, and grading exams. In the use of "realistic" for purposes of this book, it is defined as standards being high enough to motivate students to do their best, but not so high that they lose interest or can never achieve them.

The year may begin with excitement and high expectations for teachers and students but inevitably, some kids fall behind and others never quite achieve. Communication skills must be sharpened if the teacher is to help students make the year successful and stay focused. Culturally responsive pedagogy consists of the following characteristics for teachers. The teacher should:

- Have high expectations for students of all backgrounds to achieve their highest potential
- Use high level teaching strategies and encourage intellectual rigor
- Make explicit issues of power and privilege
- Incorporate students' cultures into the curriculum
- Provide opportunities for students to engage, cooperate, and collaborate with each other
- Model and demonstrate that all cultures have value
- Sustain a commitment to multicultural education throughout the year and throughout curricula, not just certain days or months of the year

A list of expectations needs to be posted in the classroom. Being specific about the expectations but discussing and posting them in kid-friendly language ensures complete clarification of what the teacher wants.

Meeting the high expectations set by the teacher is an opportunity to offer praise as a positive reinforcement. Praise should be used only in response to accomplishments and used sparingly. Another way to communicate high expectations is through the use of learning contracts. This method creates a clear commitment as to what the student is to do and achieve. These terms of the contract should be negotiated as to what work will be accepted and thus results in better buy-in by students as to the objectives and learning process and allows the teacher to ensure that the expectation agreed upon is held high.

Rubrics are another necessary tool in communicating high expectations. Discussing, creating, and examining the rubric with students in class at the time the assignment is given solidifies the expectations and allows for any misunderstood element to be clarified.

Communicating to students positive and high expectations can occur in several ways, the most obvious and powerful being through personal relationships teachers build with students. Successful youth reflect that being respected and having their strengths and abilities recognized makes them closer to their teachers (McLaughlin et al., 1994). Validating students' cultures in both what they are taught and how they are taught empowers students when combined with a wider transformative purpose.

In order to do this, teachers must spend time looking for individual student's strengths and interests and use them to promote learning in their classroom. Building this relationship can internalize high expectations in students and by doing so, develop self-esteem and self-efficiency that results in successful schools.

As Porter and Samovar (1991) have stated, "what we talk about; how we talk about it; what we see, attend to or ignore; how we think; and what we think about" (p. 21) are influenced by culture. Teachers need to be able to decipher the intellectual thought of students from different ethnic groups to teach these diverse students more effectively.

FOUR CONDITIONS NECESSARY FOR CULTURALLY RESPONSIVE TEACHING

Wlodkowski and Ginsberg (1995) state there are four conditions necessary for culturally responsive teaching. They are:

1. Establish Inclusion: The purpose of what is being learned and its relationship to the students' experience should be emphasized. Through collaboration and cooperation, students and teachers share ownership of knowing. All students are treated equitably and encouraged to point out behaviors or practices that discriminate. Examples: collaborative learning approaches, cooperative learning, writing groups, peer teaching, multidimensional sharing, focus groups, and reframing.
2. Develop Positive Attitude: Students' previous knowledge and experience relate to teaching and learning activities. Students are encouraged to use their experiences, values, needs, and strengths to make choices in content and assessment methods. Examples: Clear learning goals, problem-solving goals, fair and clear criteria of evaluation, relevant learning models, learning contracts, approaches based on multiple intelligences theory, and experiential learning.
3. Enhance Meaning: Learning experiences are challenging and include higher-order thinking and critical inquiry relevant to real-world issues in an action-oriented manner in which discussion incorporates student dialect into classroom dialogue. Examples: critical questioning, guided reciprocal peer questioning, posing problems, decision making, investigation of definitions, historical investigations, experimental inquiry, invention, art simulations, and case study methods.

4. Engender Competence: The assessment process needs to be connected to the students' world, frame of reference, and values. Examples: feedback, contextualized assessment, authentic assessment tasks, portfolios and process-folios, tests and testing formats critiqued for bias, and self-assessment.

Culturally responsive teaching is not "another thing to do." It is a teaching style or method that can be integrated into curriculum and instruction that is already taking place while increasing student self-confidence and easing the transition of diversity for all.

Chapter Two

Supporting the Teacher

"Education must be not only a transmission of culture, but also a provider of alternative views of the world and a strengthener of the will to explore them."

—*Jerome Bruner*

When language and culture of a student's home does not closely correspond to that of school, the child may be at a disadvantage in their learning cycle. The result can include the student becoming alienated and eventually completely disengaging in learning. People from different cultures learn in different ways and have different expectations of education. Children are no exception. Teachers need to gain knowledge of the cultures represented in their classrooms and create lessons and activities that are formatted in ways that are familiar to the students.

There are four cultural components. The first is communication (language and symbols): The core of all cultures is language and the backbone of symbolic interaction is symbols. Symbols can be unique to various cultures and therefore teachers need to correctly understand and interpret them. Pictorial symbols are seen in everyday life in the forms of traffic signs which convey a message.

Examples include pictures of students located at school crosswalks, or "no smoking" signs with a picture of a cigarette with a diagonal line through it.

The second component is cognitive ideas (ideas, knowledge and beliefs, values, and account). These are necessary to organize stimulus and use mental representation to link ideas into larger systems of information, thus leading to knowledge. Information of facts or assumptions that are able to be passed down from one generation to another define knowledge. The acceptance of beliefs as facts true in nature are often influenced by government, religion, or science rather than proven fact from direct experiences. Guidelines for social living are what we know as values. In cultural terms, they are the standards for what we believe is desirable, good, and beautiful. Justifying, explaining, or rationalizing defines the term accounts in which people use language to legitimize behavior toward themselves or others.

The third component is considered a major element known as behavioral. These include norms such as mores, laws, folkways, or rituals and their purpose is to determine how we act. Most are familiar with the term norms which are considered the rules and expectations set by a particular society to serve as guides to the behavior of its members. Sometimes norms vary in terms of the degree of importance which causes them to change over a period of time. Norms are usually broken down into reinforcement by sanction in the form of rewards and consequences. Customary behavior patterns which have taken form of moralistic values are an example of norms known as mores. Laws are formal important norms that translate into legal formalizations. Behavioral patterns of a particular society that are repetitive and organized are known as folkways. Highly scripted ceremonies of interactions which follow a sequence of actions are rituals, for example, baptisms, holidays, weddings.

The last component is the material component. This involves humans creating objects or materials for practical use or artistic reasons. This allows for individual cultures to express many characteristics of the society.

As with most educational resources, how the teacher implements the program determines the success of curriculum. In-service training is most effective when the training provided is:

1. Specifically designed for the curriculum to be implemented
2. Teachers are given ample opportunity for hands-on practice
3. On-site observation and feedback are provided by a supportive mentor over an extended period of time
4. Teachers are encouraged to reflect on and evaluate their new practices (Bowman, Donovan, & Burns, 2001).

PROFESSIONAL DEVELOPMENT ACTIVITIES THAT FOCUS ON CULTURAL RESPONSIVENESS

High-quality professional development opportunities that address how to effectively instruct culturally diverse students are limited for educators. This results in the majority of teachers feeling unprepared to address issues that culturally and linguistically diverse students face. These students have historically also been taught by teachers without appropriate teaching credentials and/or with little classroom experience (Rumberger & Gandara, 2004).

Few states have implemented policies or standards for teacher preparation and credential certification that specifically address diverse populations (Ardila-Rey, 2008, p. 341). This creates concern in that teacher preparation institutions involved with ongoing professional development are responsible to prepare educators who have competencies to work effectively with diverse students (Anstrom, 2004). However, despite continuing efforts to attract a balanced representation of teachers for various cultures, there is minimal diversity among teachers and the numbers who do exist are dwindling. Gay (2002) states that it is increasingly a cross-cultural occurrence that teachers are frequently not of the same race, ethnicity, class, and language dominance as their students. This demographic and cultural divide is becoming even more apparent as the number of individuals in teacher preparation and active classroom teaching dwindles (p. 1).

Student learning can be enhanced by focusing on improving the instruction practices of teachers through effective professional development. This must be supplemented with providing active learning opportunities, regularly occurring in interactive environments among teachers and providing opportunities for regular feedback (Palardy & Rumberger, 2008).

Instead of conventional teacher training that consists of one-time meetings or all-day workshops, professional development sessions need to include classroom visits throughout the year as well as development activities that apply what teachers have learned in the classroom.

When changes in instructional practices occur and are sustained, teachers have experienced intrinsic motivation and transformational learning. Instructors of adults need to serve as cultural activists who promote agency among teachers through the use of transformative learning theory. According to Ginsberg (2011), such instructors strive to facilitate the authority of teachers, keeping in mind four pedagogical principles:

1. Introduce a relevant experience, prior or current, that solicits learners' interest and desire to make meaning.
2. Collaborate with learners and use critical self-reflection to consider the information and ideas generated.
3. Facilitate reflective discourse, a discussion in which learners are able to redefine meaning for themselves based on the reciprocal sharing of information and insights with peers.
4. Initiate effective action determined in concert with learners.

Relevant experiences in which positive mutual regard is established in order to teach students more effectively is achieved when teachers visit the homes of their diverse student groups. During these visits, the educator looks for strengths in student families in order to create a curriculum that matters to the students. By experiencing the cultural conditions and emotional realities of their students, the home visit provides the teacher with real-world everyday life understanding.

Teachers can also keep a journal to critically reflect on their experience. Their writing creates an opportunity to examine their own underlying beliefs and assumptions in order to generate their own meaning of these experiences. This also allows teachers the opportunity to engage in a dialogue with peers and to search for a clearer understanding and interpretation of their experience. Allowing teachers the chance to experience and create self-generated knowledge (generated by teachers, not told to them by an outside professional development specialist), they are more inclined to use their own agency to explore possibilities for changing teaching and curricula as ways to take effective action.

When teachers experience something that is relevant and disorienting and have the time and support to understand their feelings and to gain insight into their personal and professional beliefs, they are at a place conducive to becoming more competent in their instruction through culturally responsive teaching (Ginsberg, 2001).

ENSURING ALL FACULTY RESPECTS THE CULTURE OF THEIR STUDENTS

Culture plays a key role in shaping our values, attitudes, and beliefs. Because of this, it is an intrinsic part of who we are and how we identify ourselves. It molds our experiences as well as how we interpret life's defining moments. Everyone, including classroom teachers, school administrators, and policymakers, carries their cultural experiences and perspectives into their everyday decisions and actions—educational and personal—and so do students from various ethnic and cultural backgrounds (Gay, 2000).

Cultural competence is built upon effectively serving students from diverse cultures. According to NEA (2008) four skill areas must exist for basic cultural competence. These skill areas can apply to individual educators, the schools where they work, and the education system as a whole.

1. Various cultural backgrounds, communication differences, traditions, and customs need to be respected and accepted if diversity is to be valued.
2. All educators bring their own cultures, experiences, background knowledge, beliefs, values, and interests with them that define their place in the family, school, and society. They must be aware that these cultural characteristics also define how they will interact with students.
3. The many dynamics involved in cultural interactions must be understood, as it is within this understanding of the various factors such as historical experiences and relationships be-

tween the cultures in a community that educators gain a sense of cultural value.
4. The learning environment needs to be adapted to better serve the diversity in today's classrooms. This can be done by using the knowledge of various cultures as the basis for educational services offered.

Talking, thinking, and learning must be taking place regularly if effective teaching is in place. No one person can possibly know everything about all cultures. Today's technology presents the opportunity to utilize research, participate in relevant professional development, and show educators how to develop new ways of using cultural strengths to improve learning. Parents are also another great source of cultural information. Teachers should make every effort for parents to feel welcome by inviting them to participate as speakers and volunteers as often as possible.

All good teachers have the ability to build a bridge between what the student knows and what they need to learn. Although this is common knowledge, one detail left out of debates about what makes an effective teacher is the process of embracing students' cultural backgrounds. Culturally responsive teaching often requires confronting some of the most painful divides in American life (Quinton, 2013).

If the time is not taken by an educator to learn and find out about their students' everyday life experiences, their dialects, their cultural backgrounds, or their families, the manner in which they teach will be based on instructional styles from their own experiences. Culturally responsive teaching is not lowering standards, but the focus is targeted on creating a link between home and school to strengthen the community and understanding of various cultures' value. By inviting parents to speak about their culture or profession or have students critically think about articles or text and explore them for cultural bias, it deepens understanding and better prepares students for the real world.

VALUE AND CELEBRATE CULTURE

If our educational system truly is for all students, then differentiated instruction must be provided to ensure students feel they are included. This is not accomplished by merely being tolerant, but by providing a link between feeling included and academic achievement. Students learn much quicker in an environment in which they feel included and able to relax (Haynes, 2007).

Including one cultural day in the curriculum is not an effective way to build students' cultural knowledge. Educators must integrate lessons and activities that convey a variety of multicultural perspectives. Today's diverse students need teachers to move beyond the surface level and work to both understand and teach cultural information.

The individual and personal accounts along with real-life experiences need to be celebrated in today's diverse classrooms. One resource that can provide a springboard for ideas to accomplish this is found at http://www.appreciatediversitymonth.org. This website shares eighty-eight ways to celebrate and appreciate diversity. The activities are divided into eight categories including arts, business, connections, education, food, history, outreach, and traditions. These activities can be:

1. Individual experiences or group events (done in pairs, small groups, or even through the Web-based conversation bulletin board on the Web site)
2. Magnified or minimized based on the audience

3. A single event or a series of events done over time
4. Enhanced with facilitated dialogues that promote "conversations of connection"
5. Communicated through a variety of vehicles, such as handouts, index cards, or follow-up emails

Some activity examples include:

- Cultural Art Exhibit

    Description: Feature the work of artists of various cultures and backgrounds. Include signage that tells the story of the art and the artist. If enough local artists, invite the artists to join one or more of the showings to share their perspectives.

    Connection Activity: View the art at least with one other person so at the conclusion of the viewing you can talk about what your individual experiences were like.

- Cultural Values Conversations

    Description: Have a discussion with someone from another culture about their cultural values related to various cultural variables like time, gestures, appearance, and how they view the elderly. Use a resource book like *Gestures: The Do's and Taboos of Body Language around the World* or *Bridging Cultural Conflicts: A New Approach for a Changing World* to inspire ideas.

    Connection Activity: Think about a time when you have been frustrated, misread, or misunderstood something because of your own personal expectations around time, appearance, or gestures. Start your conversation with a nonjudgmental question like, "Does your culture tend to . . . ? or "How are elders in your culture viewed?"

- Life Events Photo Board

    Description: Create a corkboard display related to students' personal, important life events, such as weddings, births, Bar/Bat Mitzvahs, Quinceañera, family reunions, etc.

    Connection Activity: Ask students to share photos or other paper memorabilia.

TAKE AWAY BARRIERS THAT IMPEDE PROGRESS

The effect of politics is evident in the unequal funding determined by the economic class of the students served in our schools. This attitude is also present in the use of grading and tracking policies as well as the physical conditions of classrooms and buildings. For this reason, many teachers, administrators, and parents view their school's increasing diversity as a problem rather than an incredible opportunity.

According to AACTE (1999) Colleges of Education programs are graduating a significant number of white female teachers (87 percent white; 74 percent female) which results in 90 percent of public school teachers being white and as little as 7 percent being African American (Synder, 1999). If schools and faculties do not acknowledge the need for culturally competent teachers in today's classrooms, the resistance will increase, resulting in children from ethnically and linguistically diverse backgrounds continually being underserved or unserved. Teaching styles and content of instruction need to be adapted by teachers but many are unsure how to accomplish this in order to be responsive to student values and cultural norms. DeSherbinin (2004) recognizes the disconnect that occurs "when faculties that are overwhelmingly 'white' are expected to be effective teachers and mentors for students of color who hail from ethnic or socioeconomic backgrounds unfamiliar to middle class white academics."

Helping staff to develop a culturally responsive pedagogy can assist in fostering active thinking, intellectual engagement, and democratic participation based on student perspectives and backgrounds. Collaboration between all faculty members allows sharing of stories that detail the interaction within a society where the focus is race and class.

For these reasons, unequal educational attainment among students is no coincidence. Michael Fullan (2002) suggests that levels of multidimensional change in schools require three components for successful implementation:

1. Revised material
2. Revised practices
3. (Most important) revised beliefs

A great resource for materials to train staff can be found at http://www.whatsrace.org/pages.html. This Web site provides sample agendas, discussion questions, tips for effective facilitation, and a list of suggested follow-up action steps for different groups on cultural responsiveness and identifying the barriers that they may not have realized exist. The activities are designed at three different levels depending on the faculty needs:

1. Low risk: containing trust-building activities and icebreakers which help to foster an inclusive atmosphere.

2. Medium risk: helping to uncover existing disparities and help staff connect issues raised by a video to a larger social context.
3. High risk: helps teachers explore their personal stake or vantage point by putting them in another's shoes. These activities are designed to expose blind spots or sensitivities.

The rapidly growing demographics of U.S. schools demand that educators engage in a vigorous, ongoing, and systematic process of professional development to prepare all educators to function effectively in a highly diverse and demanding environment. A transformation in schools is desperately needed. Blame and excuses are no longer viable as schools are forced to transform in order to serve all students well.

Chapter Three

Learning Within the Context of Culture

"Preservation of one's own culture does not require contempt or disrespect for other cultures."
—Cesar Chavez

Vygotsky (1962) examined how social environments affected the learning process. He stated that learning takes place through interactions students have with their peers as well as other individuals. This learning ability can be maximized when the teacher creates a learning environment in which students interact with each other through discussion, collaboration, and feedback. Vygotsky (1962) also emphasized that culture is the primary determining factor for knowledge construction. This means that individuals learn through a cultural lens in which they interact with others and follow the rules, skills, and abilities shaped by their culture.

Today's teachers need to use instructional strategies that promote literacy across the curriculum. Opportunities for students to discuss their learning must also be evident. This discussion must have a purpose that includes comments that build off one another in a meaningful exchange not only between students but also between the teacher and students to promote deeper understanding.

CULTURAL COMPONENTS:

Researchers differ on how many components culture entails. One view is supported by Damen (1987) who presents six characteristics of culture:

1. Culture is learned
2. Cultures and cultural patterns change
3. Culture is a universal fact of human life
4. Culture provides sets of unique and interrelated, selected blueprints for living and accompanying sets of values and beliefs to support those blueprints
5. Language and culture are closely related and interactive
6. Culture functions as a filtering device between its bearers and the great range of stimuli presented by the environment

Additionally, Damen suggested that culture can be examined from the point of view of its individual components (such as dress, systems of rewards and punishments, uses of time and space, fashions of eating, means of communication, family relationships, beliefs and values) or from the more social point of view of its systems (such as kinship, education, economy, government association, and health). Below is a more detailed description of each:

1. **Language and Communication Style**: Wide variety of verbal and nonverbal patterns and behaviors including social customs about who speaks to whom
2. **Health Beliefs**: Range of assumptions about the causes of disease as well as the proper remedies for illness
3. **Family Relationships**: Primary unit of society, in it, children are socialized into human society and into culture's particular

beliefs, attitudes, values, and behaviors. Family relationships include family structure, roles, dynamics, and expectations

4. **Sexuality**: Enables people to feel good about how their bodies look and feel. It allows them to enjoy the pleasure their bodies can give to them and others. The need to be touched in loving ways. The feeling of physical attraction for another person, body image, and fantasy are all a part of sensuality

5. **Gender Roles:** What is considered appropriate and acceptable behavior for men and women

6. **Religion**: Specific set of beliefs and practices regarding the spiritual realm and beyond the visible world

7. **Level of Acculturation**: Process that occurs when two separate cultural groups come in contact with each other and change occurs in at least one of the two groups

8. **Immigration Status**: Whether or not an individual is classified as a refugee, an immigrant, or an undocumented (illegal). How one is labeled by the U.S. government has important implications for the kinds of services one can expect

9. **Political Power**: Group's level of formal involvement in local, state, and national government as well as in informal advocacy organization

10. **Racism:** Prejudice + Power = Racism. Prejudice is unreasonable feelings, opinions, and attitudes especially of a hostile nature directed against any group

11. **Poverty and Economic Concerns**: Ties to racism in this country. Particularly the assumption that all poor people are African American or Latino. It is not true; highest percent is white

12. **History of Oppression**: Government policies harmful to racial and ethnic groups in U.S. history such as: anti-mixed race

marriage laws, forced removal of Native Americans from their land, internment of Japanese during WWII, and Jim Crow laws regarding education of African Americans

An important component of effective culturally responsive classrooms is the use of a range of instructional methods (Bromley, 1998). Varying and adapting methods that are tailored to suit the setting, the students, and the subject increases the chances that students will succeed. Using a variety of instructional strategies and learning activities can provide students with opportunities to learn in ways that are responsive to their own communication styles and aptitudes. Some examples are:

a. Use cooperative learning especially for material new to the students
b. Assign independent work after students are familiar with concept
c. Use role-playing strategies
d. Assign students research projects that focus on issues or concepts that apply to their own community or cultural group
e. Provide various options for completing an assignment

BRIDGE CULTURAL DIFFERENCES THROUGH EFFECTIVE COMMUNICATION

Today's classroom evidence shows the range of students represented across cultures and age groups and reinforces the need for changes across the curriculum. Using these processes, student achievement and self-esteem at all levels results in gains in both developmental and cultural perspectives related to identity and learning.

Focusing on the transmission of information in the learning design can result in long-term ineffectiveness. It is viewed as an active and recursive process by most contemporary views. Learning context is pivotal in knowledge construction and understanding and is what drives the perspective of constructivist learning. This learning style is grounded in the belief that learning and cognition are most effective when used in a meaningful context as well as within the community and culture in which learners live. Prior knowledge and beliefs are used by learners to make sense of new ideas and experiences they encounter in school.

The constructivist view of learning is one in which there is a process of developing understanding through problem solving and critical reflection. As an active process, learning is most effective and efficient when learners are engaged in what is known as *learning by doing*. Students' thinking is as important as the products of that thinking in classrooms guided by constructivist principles. Within these principles, a student's problem-solving process is as important as the solutions that result from it. Villegas and Lucas (2002) state that a constructivist education is more likely to prepare children to fulfill their roles in a democratic society than an education that is rooted in conventional thinking (p. 76).

Teachers' main goal should be to support students' construction of knowledge and help them build bridges between what they know and believe about a topic as well as new ideas and experiences they are exposed to. This takes the form of questioning, interpreting, and analyzing information which is used in the context of problems or issues relevant to students. Following the constructivist view of learning, curriculum should be anchored in the following reasons according to Villegas and Lucas (2002):

1. All students are depicted as capable learners who continuously strive to make sense of new ideas. By acknowledging that diversity plays a central role in learning, constructivism places a responsibility on educators to adjust standard school practices to the diverse backgrounds of their students.
2. Constructivist teaching promotes critical thinking, problem solving, collaboration, and the recognition of multiple perspectives.
3. Emphasizing higher-order thinking and problem solving, constructivists' classrooms promote academic rigor to a greater extent than transmission classrooms which rely largely on recall of information.

Unless prospective teachers experience the knowledge construction process as learners, they are not likely to adopt constructivist views of education or use constructivist strategies in their own teaching (Feiman-Nemser & Melnick, 1992).

North Americans' approach to business is very much a "my way or the highway" mentality. Americans tend to think that once foreigners are living and working in this country, they should immediately change their ways to be more "American." But as Herzog, Schlottmann, and Johnson (1986) point out, "A lot of the labor force is foreign-born or first generation American, which means that there are still strong connections to the cultural norms and styles." The expectation that other cultures should immediately forget their upbringing and adopt our North American ways is unrealistic.

As with the labor force, there are no specific teaching techniques to make diverse students feel that they belong in a new culture, but as successful educators, there are ways for you to make them feel welcome in your classroom. In today's society, people from all cultures are better able to appreciate and accept the diversity of not only their own heritage, but also others that are similar and different to which they are exposed.

Students also need to strengthen their appreciation of individual differences which will lessen the desire to make fun of those with various differing beliefs. The best way to understand others is to step into their shoes. Learning is more effective when the student has lived it, felt it, and experienced it. Some useful strategies include:

Learn their names

Take the time to learn how to pronounce students' names correctly. Ask them to say their name. Listen carefully and repeat it until you know it. If a student's name is Pedro, make sure you do not call him /peedro/ or Peter. Also, model the correct pronunciation of students' names to the class so that all students can say the correct pronunciation. This is the first step in knowing who your students are. Using their name communicates respect, helps them feel recognized as individuals, and helps to draw out and include shy students in class discussions. A few ways to implement this are:

- Have students wear nametags, or have them write their first names on the front and back of tented index cards on their desktops.
- Schedule a set time during the day and have the students introduce themselves to their neighbors. An extension of this activity would be to then have each student introduce a neighbor to the class, along with one interesting fact about him or her.

- Take a photo of each student. Write the student's name on the photo and keep them as a reference or you can post them in the room for other students to reference.
- Have students create "business cards"—using a 4x6-inch index card. Include some specific information about themselves such as a brief bio, something they are an expert about, and other strengths they have. They can then share these in small groups or a "show and tell" and then you can collect them to learn more about your students.

Offer one-on-one assistance when possible

Some culturally diverse students may not answer voluntarily in class or ask for your help even if they need it. Some may smile and nod, but this does not necessarily mean that they understand. Go over to their desk to offer individual coaching in a friendly way.

Assign a peer partner

Identify a classmate who really wants to help culturally diverse students. This student can make sure that the other understands what he or she is supposed to do. It will be even more helpful if the peer partner knows the culture or first language.

Post a visual daily schedule

Even if some of the students do not yet understand all of the words that you speak, it is possible for them to understand the structure of each day. Whether through chalkboard art or images on Velcro, you can post the daily schedule each morning. By writing down times and having pictures next to words like lunch, wash hands, math, and field trip, all students regardless of language can have a general sense of the upcoming day.

Use an interpreter

Although budget constraints make this difficult, having on-site interpreters can be very helpful in smoothing out misunderstandings that arise due to communication problems and cultural differences. If an on-site interpreter (a paid or volunteer school staff position) is not available, try to find an adult—perhaps another parent who is familiar with the school or "knows the system"—who is willing to serve this purpose. In difficult situations, it would not be appropriate for another child to translate.

Students can make unintentional "mistakes" as they are trying hard to adjust to a new cultural setting. They are constantly transferring what they know as acceptable behaviors from their own culture to the U.S. classroom and school. Be patient as students learn English and or cultural norms and adjust.

Invite their culture into the classroom

Encourage students to share their language and culture with you and your class. Show-and-tell is a good opportunity for diverse students to bring in something representative of their culture, if they wish. They could also tell a popular story or folktale using words, pictures, gestures, and movements. The students could also try to teach the class some words from their native language.

Use materials related to your students' cultures

Children respond when they see books, topics, characters, and images that are familiar. Try to achieve a good balance of books and materials that include different cultures.

Label classroom objects

Labeling classroom objects will allow students from different cultures to better understand their immediate surroundings. These labels will also assist you when explaining or giving directions. Start with everyday items and build as you go.

Include diverse students in a nonthreatening manner

Students from different cultural backgrounds may be apprehensive about speaking out in a group. They might be afraid to make mistakes in front of their peers. Their silence could also be a sign of respect for you as an authority—and not a sign of their inability or refusal to participate. Find ways to involve these students in a nonthreatening way. Asking students their preference is a good starting point.

Involve all students in cooperative learning

Some students are used to working cooperatively on assigned tasks. What may look like cheating to you is actually a culturally acquired learning style—an attempt to mimic, see, or model what has to be done. Use this cultural trait as a plus in your classroom. Assign buddies or peer tutors so that diverse students are able to participate in all class activities.

Help your culturally diverse students follow established rules

All students need to understand and follow your classroom rules from the very beginning, and students from various cultural backgrounds are no exception. Teach them your classroom management rules as soon as possible to avoid misunderstandings, discipline problems, and feelings of low self-esteem. Here are a few strategies that you can use in class:

- Use visuals like pictures, symbols, and reward systems to communicate your expectations in a positive and direct manner.
- Physically model language to students in classroom routines and instructional activities. Students will need to see you or their peers model behavior when you want them to sit down, walk to the bulletin board, work with a partner, copy a word, etc.
- Be consistent and fair with all students. Once students from various cultures clearly understand what is expected, hold them equally accountable for their behavior.

INTERPRETING NONVERBAL LANGUAGE ACROSS CULTURES

McGee (2008) states that spoken words are only one way to communicate in everyday conversation. As little as 7 percent of a message may be expressed in words while tone of voice accounts for 38 percent and body language accounts for 55 percent of an overall message. Understanding nonverbal messages may be difficult because different cultures have different expectations about eye contact, physical touch, body gestures, etc. A person's gender, age, position in society, level of acculturation, and individual preferences can complicate communication even more.

To start, the definition of body language as used for this purpose includes all forms of nonverbal communication. Examples include, how we greet each other, how we sit or stand, facial expressions, our clothes, hairstyles, tone of voice, eye movements, how we listen to each other, how we breathe, how close one stands to others, and how one touches others. "The misuse of body language can be an unpleasant or even dangerous experience for message encoders" (Rugsaken, 2006).

Argyle (1978) states humans have more than 700,000 forms of body language. It is no wonder that not only educators have such misconceptions of behaviors of students, but also that the students have misconceptions about the teacher and their actions as well. These are just a few examples, from various researchers, as to how body language is interpreted across cultures:

Head: In most societies, a nodding head signifies agreement or approval. But in some cultures, like parts of Greece, Yugoslavia, Bulgaria, and Turkey, a nodding head means no. In most Asian cultures head is where spirit resides and one should not touch another's head.

Face: Facial expressions reflect emotional feelings and attitudes. While expressing true feeling and emotion is valued in the West, it is prohibited in the East. The Asians who are taught to practice self-control are often labeled as "emotionless" and of possessing mixed-up emotions. Smiling in the East is not necessarily a sign of happiness, rather it signifies yes, I don't understand what you said, or can be a cover-up for embarrassment. Northern Europeans as a group smile with much less frequency, reserving the expression to show felt happiness.

Eyes: While good eye contact is praised and expected in the West, it is seen as a sign of disrespect and challenge in other cultures including Asian, Latino, and African where the less eye contact these groups have with an individual, the more respect they show. For Muslims, direct eye contact between members of the opposite sex is considered bold and flirtatious. Arabs have greater eye contact than Americans among members of the same gender.

Southern Europeans generally engage in more eye contact than Americans, but Britains engage in less.

Closing Eyes: In the Japanese culture one closes their eyes in order to close out everything else in order to digest what they are listening to.

Nose: Tapping the nose is more common in Europe than in the United States. It means confidential in England but watch out in Italy. Blowing the nose on public streets, while seen as an impolite gesture in North America, is commonplace in most Asian countries. This rids the body of waste and therefore it is seen as healthy. At the same time, Asians do not understand why the Americans blow their nose onto a Kleenex that is put back in their pocket and carried with them throughout the day.

Lips and Mouth: Kissing is a sign of love or affection in the West. People kiss when they meet or when they say goodbye. But kissing is viewed as an intimate act in Asia and is not permissible in public. In some cultures such as Filipino, Native American, Puerto Rican, and several Latin American cultures, people use their lips to point instead of a finger.

Arms: Some cultures like the Italians use their arms freely. Others like Japanese are more reserved. In Japan, it is considered impolite to gesture with broad movements of the arms.

Hands: Of all the body parts, the hands probably are used most often for communicating nonverbally. Hand waves are used for greeting, beckoning, or farewell. The American goodbye wave can be interpreted in many parts of Europe and Latin America as the signal for no. The Italian goodbye wave can be interpreted by the Americans as the gesture for "come here." The American "come here" gesture can be seen as an insult in most Asian countries where they use it for calling animals. Asians call others with a similar hand movement but with their palm down.

Handshaking: This is a common form of greeting and leave-taking in the Western culture. While it is accepted in Asia, the Asians still prefer a different form of greeting. A bow in East Asia, or a Wai (joining of two hands together like a prayer) for some southern and South Eastern Asian countries. Asians and Middle Easterners prefer a soft handshake as strong grips are interpreted as a sign of aggression.

While both right and left hands have equal status in the West, the right hand has special significance and the left hand is dirty in the East. In Middle Eastern and some Asian countries it is best to accept or offer cards or gifts with the right hand or with both. The OK sign (the thumb and the forefinger form an O) means fine or OK in most cultures. However, it means zero or worthless in France and many European countries, and in Turkey means that one is homosexual. The same signal is an insult in Greece, Brazil, Italy, and Russia. A thumbs-up sign indicates an OK or good job in most cultures, but it is an insult in Australia, New Zealand, and in most African countries. It also translates into a rude and offensive gesture in Islamic and Asian countries.

Time: The way we use time in America also sends messages without a word being spoken. In American business culture, respect is communicated through punctuality. In Latin and Middle Eastern cultures, which place high value on interpersonal relationships, respect means continuing a meeting or conversation until it reaches a natural conclusion, even if it makes you late for the next one.

Relationships with the principal, teachers, and even other parents can often be influenced by the customs and experiences families from diverse backgrounds have. Many times, these families are experiencing challenges in meeting the basic needs of food and shelter for their family; are affected by a negative experience they had in school; or may feel intimidated by school staff or the school environment. A few suggestions of how educators can assist with this are:

- Nonreading or nonspeaking parents can participate in home learning through the use of newspapers. Parents and children can look through the ads and make price comparisons, discuss the weather which is often pictorial with weekly forecasts
- Holding family math and science nights so children and parents can explore together math or science activities including games that families can play at home
- Twice a year schools may wish to dismiss students at 1pm to make time for a one-and-a-half-hour hands-on workshop for parents and their children. Topics could include language and math skill development, reading, or, if resources are available, cooking with children
- To build a trust between home and school, home-school lessons can be used to reach out to parents of different backgrounds resulting in building of trust between home and school

One very important principle to remember when communicating with parents from different cultural backgrounds is that mutual respect is present and the foundation for success in any communication.

STUDENT-CENTERED INSTRUCTION

Student-centered instruction breaks many of the traditional boundaries governing how students have been conditioned and expected to learn. It integrates student engagement, immersion, and personal responsibility. Action-oriented instructional formats promote student self-reliance (Felder & Brent, 1996), including:

- Open-ended problem solving requiring critical and creative thinking
- Role-playing and participation in stimulated situations
- Nontraditional writing assignments
- Collaborative team projects
- Individual self-paced assignments
- Community engagement

In relation to curriculum design, student centeredness includes the idea that students have choice in what to study and how to study. Student-centered instruction is a different method from the traditional teacher-centered instruction. Learning is cooperative, collaborative, and community-oriented. Students are encouraged to direct their own learning and to work with other students on research projects and assignments that are both culturally and socially relevant to them. Students become self-confident, self-directed, and proactive.

Children develop cognitively by interacting with both adults and more knowledgeable peers. These interactions allow students to hypothesize, experiment with new ideas, and receive feedback (Darling-Hammond, 1997).

Some ways to implement a student-centered instructional approach are:

1. Promote student engagement

    - Have students generate lists of topics they wish to study and/or research

- Allow students to select their own reading material

2. Share responsibility of instruction

    - Initiate cooperative learning groups (Padrón, Waxman, & Rivera, 2002)
    - Have students lead discussion groups or reteach concepts

3. Create inquiry-based, discovery-oriented curriculum

    - Create classroom projects that involve the community

4. Encourage a community of learners

    - Form book clubs or literature circles for reading discussions (Daniels, 2002)
    - Conduct student directed sharing time (Brisk & Harrington, 2000)
    - Use cooperative learning strategies such as jigsaw (Brisk & Harrington, 2000)

Culturally relevant teaching is built on the key component of what students already know. Students use knowledge needed to address relationships within and outside the classroom. Utilizing student voice is critical in every learner's experience as it requires students to be active, responsible participants in their own learning.

THE CULTURALLY RESPONSIVE CLASSROOM

According to Gray (2012), there are five ways to create a culturally responsive classroom:

1. To learn about the students, teachers must be committed to finding out about families, cultures, and interests that make up the classroom family. This can be done by talking with parents and community members, reading books, watching movies, making home visits, and developing opportunities for students to share about their family traditions and cultures.
2. Life experiences that students bring into the classroom should be built upon. Curriculum can be connected for students by using real-world examples which allow for deeper engagement that will provide clearer understanding of the community national and global identity.
3. Providing a model that emphasizes students caring for one another and being responsible for each other "both inside and outside" the classroom creates a culturally responsive learning environment. Routines should be consistent to help students feel valued and safe as well as reinforcing accountability to one another. Natural light, moveable chairs and desks with ample space to highlight student work, and cultural artifacts communicate that the classroom is for the students to create.
4. High standards and expectations assist students in reaching their goals and beyond. Students should be treated as competent and lessons should be designed with the most underserved student in mind.
5. Understand your own cultural identity, and its consequences. Rigorously examine your cultural behavior patterns, especially when it comes to classroom management and discipline. Be yourself with your students—honest, caring, and human.

The culturally responsive teaching approach views current schools' inadequacies as the primary reason for students' academic failures. Academic success is closely tied to feeling effective, intelligent, and valued and today's educators must adopt new pedagogical approaches to create such feelings in their culturally diverse students.

Chapter Four

Managing the Classroom with Cultural Responsiveness

"If you are building a culture where honest expectations are communicated and peer accountability is the norm, then the group will address poor performance and attitudes."
—Henry Cloud

WHAT IS CULTURALLY RESPONSIVE CLASSROOM MANAGEMENT?

Instituting classroom management principles has implications for the learning progress of all children, especially low-performing, poor, special education, and racial/ethnic minority children (Saphier & Gower, 1997). Culturally Responsive Classroom Management (CRCM) is a method of running a classroom with children in a way that provides a safe environment regardless of culture. CRCM is a pedagogical approach that guides the management decisions that teachers make.

Explicit instruction about the rules is one of the key principles of CRCM. Before correcting the student, the teacher needs to consider what the reason is for the misbehavior. Could it be a cultural clash, a miscommunication, or does the rule itself need to be revisited? When a student does not adhere to a rule, the teacher must use a caring fashion to explain why the behavior is not acceptable and ask the student why he or she did it. This helps the teacher to better understand how a child perceives the rules of the classroom while building relationships with the students.

Authoritarian classroom management techniques do not create a caring and nurturing bond with students as a culturally responsive classroom will. CRCM creates an environment which causes students to think twice about making poor behavior choices which may result in jeopardizing their relationship with the teacher. To build a rapport with students, teachers need to spend time on connectedness-building games the first few weeks of class including having conversations with students outside the classroom. Another strategy would be to start each class in a welcoming manner and to always remember that regardless of the behavior problems from the previous class session, students need to start with a clean slate each day. This will create an atmosphere of partnerships and result in an optimal learning environment.

The goal of CRCM for culturally responsive teachers is not just to achieve compliance or control, but to expose all students to equitable opportunities for learning. "CRCM is classroom management in the service of social justice" (Weinstein, Tomlinson-Clarke, & Curran, 2004, p. 27).

Weinstein, Tomlinson-Clarke, and Curran (2004) claim there are five concepts of culturally responsive classroom management derived from the culturally responsive pedagogy:

1. Recognition of One's Own Cultural Lens and Biases: Teachers need to explore and reflect upon where their assumptions, attitudes, and biases come from and to understand that how

they view the world can lead them to misrepresentations of behaviors and inequitable treatment of culturally different students (Weinstein et al., 2004).

There are several things teachers can do to explore belief systems:

> a. Read and discuss Peggy McIntosh's (1988) work on white and male privilege.
> b. Write a personal identity story to explore how their identities have been socially constructed and how they fit into a multicultural world (Noel, 2000).
> c. See where they fit on the cultural Proficiency Receptivity Scale (Lindsey, Roberts, & Campbell-Jones, 2005), a tool designed for self-reflection that will also enable teachers to examine the policies and practices of their school.

2. Knowledge of Students' Cultural Background: Teachers need to become knowledgeable of students' cultural background (Sheets & Gay, 1996). Gaining general knowledge about a cultural or ethnic group can give teachers a sense of views about behavior, rules of decorum and etiquette, communication and learning styles; however, you need to be careful not to form stereotypes. This knowledge can act as a firewall against inappropriate referrals to special education. Teachers may:

> a. Form study groups to read culturally responsive literature that reflects the identities of the students in their classroom.

      b. Work with the students to develop family history projects in which students explore their cultural backgrounds and share them with the class.

      c. Conduct home visits and consult with parents and community members to gain insight. Some areas may include; family background and structure, education, discipline, religion, food, health, hygiene, history, traditions, and holidays (Weinstein et al., 2004).

3. Awareness of the Broader, Social, Economic, and Political Context: The current policies and practices in discipline of today's classrooms oftentimes discriminate against certain children. Unfortunately, a misjudgment like this has potential of labeling a student behavior and resulting in the teacher's request for a special education referral. Current real-world issues need to be discussed not only between the teachers, but also between the teacher and students.

      a. Form a study circle to examine structures and policies and whether they are fair to everyone. They can look at what they see as inappropriate student behavior and discuss if they actually are incidents of student resistance to what they see as an unfair system (Weinstein et al., 2004).

      b. Create critical/social justice classroom grounded in the lives of children that involves dialogue, questioning/problem posing, critiquing bias and attitudes, and teaching activism for social justice (Peterson, 1994).

4. Ability and Willingness to Use Culturally Appropriate Management Strategies: Reflect on the ways that classroom management practices promote or obstruct equal access to learning. Creating a physical setting that supports academic and social goals, establishing and maintaining expectations for behavior and working with families (Weinstein et al., 2004). Through the lens of cultural diversity, decision making about the environment is filtered when a teacher is culturally responsive. Respect for diversity is the primary thought process using the physical environment. Some samples of this are using:

   a. World maps that highlight students' countries of origin
   b. Signs or banners can welcome students in different languages they speak
   c. Posters depicting people of various cultural groups
   d. Children's individual photos can be mounted on poster board and used to create a jigsaw puzzle
   e. Desks arranged in clusters allow students to work together on activities

Clear expectations also need to be established by the teacher so students better understand acceptable behavior (Weiner, 2003). The teacher can do this by:

   a. Engaging students in discussions about the class norms
   b. Modeling the behavior that is expected
   c. Providing opportunities for students to practice

5. Commitment to Building Caring Classroom Communities: Students often make decisions of what they do in class based on their perception of whether or not the teacher cares about them (Weinstein et al., 2004). Poor classroom management threatens school connectedness because poorly managed classrooms cannot provide a stable environment for respectful and meaningful student learning (Blum, 2005).

For effective classroom management and to better enhance learning, good teacher-student relationships are key (Marzano, Marzano & Pickering 2003). Anything done to show interest in students as individuals will have a positive impact on learning. Teachers can:

a. Greet students outside of school such as at extracurricular activities or the store
b. Single out a few students every day in the lunchroom and talk to them
c. Be aware of and comment on important events in the students' lives such as sports and drama

The use of positive behavior not only supports the identification of environmental events, circumstances, and interactions that may trigger problem behaviors, but also develops strategies and new skills to address them.

CULTURALLY MEDIATED INSTRUCTION

Culturally mediated instruction incorporates all student learning styles and backgrounds into classroom instruction. The primary focus is based on differentiated instruction that integrates various cultural elements into the learning environment. In this model, instruction provides students with a culturally rich learning environment that implements diverse ways of knowing, understanding, and representing information in order to encourage multicultural viewpoints.

Many students of color have an understanding of negative images of their race and have come to internalize them (Gay, 2000). The results of these negative images which are often promoted by larger society is reflected in their school performance (Noguera, 2003). Schools have a unique opportunity to be able to help students interpret and interrupt this imagery by providing interactions with curriculum through hiring teachers who will validate their culture. Tatum (2003) detailed an oppositional identity development where Black students were forced to choose between affirming their culture and achieving academic success. When their culture was not present, Black students felt that academic success was not part of being Black. In contrast, when students see their culture represented in the curriculum they are much more likely to have higher self-concept, resulting in them being more open with others and to learning (Gay, 2000).

When instruction incorporates and integrates diverse ways of understanding and representing information, it is culturally mediated. In this type of environment, learning takes place in an encouraging way where multicultural viewpoints allow for the incorporation of knowledge that is relevant to students. Learning is developed within social settings and relationships among students and those between teacher and students develop around students' cultures.

When teachers do not consider students' culture or personal characteristics, but are concerned with ensuring that students "fit into society," it is an assimilationist teaching style that causes them to "homogenize" students into one American identity (Ladson-Billings, 1997, p.

38). The context of a concept needs to be taken into consideration for cultural responsiveness to be effective. The aim of culturally responsive pedagogy is to empower students intellectually, socially, emotionally, and politically by using cultural relevance to impart knowledge, skills, and attitudes (Ladson-Billings, 1997, p. 20).

TEACHER AS FACILITATOR

The role of today's teacher is changing. Where instruction used to be very teacher-centered, teachers now act as guides, mediators, consultants, instructors, and advocates to develop a learning environment that is relevant and reflective of their students. Therefore, time must be given by the facilitator to formulate a learning plan. No longer can the excuse of standardized testing requirements be used to neglect incorporating learning opportunities that are culturally diverse. Teachers need to ask, "What are those things that my students need to know and what activities can I use that will create real understanding for them?" In doing so, learning moves toward understanding, and away from rote memorization. Objectives should be clear and functional as well as based on what the teacher wants the learner to do. Through the development of good objectives and strong essential questions, the teacher transitions into the role of facilitator. Additionally, assessment questions need to ask the learner to assess and internalize what they know about a subject, not just how pick from a few select answer choices.

This helps students and staff effectively connect their culture and community-based knowledge to enhance classroom learning experiences. Langdon (2009) suggests the following in how to do this:

1. Learn about student cultures

    a. Have students share artifacts from home that reflect their culture
    b. Have students write about traditions shared by their families
    c. Have students research different aspects of their culture

2. Vary teaching approaches to accommodate diverse learning styles and language proficiency

    a. Initiate cooperative learning groups (Padrón, Waxman, & Rivera, 2002)
    b. Have students participate in book clubs (Daniels, 2002)
    c. Use student-directed discussion groups (Brisk & Harrington, 2000)
    d. Speak in ways that meet the comprehension and language development needs of ELLs (Yedlin, 2004)

3. Utilize various resources in the students' communities

    a. Have members of the community speak to students on various subjects
    b. Ask members of the community to teach a lesson or give a demonstration in their field of expertise to the students
    c. Invite parents to the classroom to show students alternative ways of approaching a problem

When the rules of the classroom culture are made explicit while also enabling students to compare and contrast with other cultures, teachers are promoting critical thinking. In order for this to effectively be implemented, teachers must make the classroom an effective learning environment through their attitudes, knowledge, and skills. As the opportunities for students to participate in learning communities increases, students will be better able to assume constructive roles as workers, family members, and citizens in a global society.

BUILDING A LEARNING COMMUNITY

According to the Center for the Integration of Research, Teaching, and Learning (CIRTL, 2013), "learning communities bring people together for shared learning, discovery, and the generation of knowledge." All individual participants come together in a learning community and take responsibility for achieving throughout all areas of learning goals. Learning goals can either be very specific to individual courses and activities or they can be a guide to an entire teaching and learning enterprise.

The following four core ideas are central to the learning community process (CIRTL, 2013):

- Shared discovery and learning. Participants learn more when they share responsibility in a collaborative learning activity. As opposed to an "expert-centered" lecture form, collaborative learning techniques allow students to see that their contributions are included in the learning goals.
- Functional connections among learners. When the interactions among learners are meaningful, learning communities will develop. These interactions must also be functional in order for the

work within the learning activity to be accomplished. The connections become meaningful when they extend throughout the entire learning community which includes students, faculty, and staff members.
- Connections to other related learning and life experiences. When implicit and explicit connections are made to real-world experiences and prior knowledge, learning communities excel. This helps the learner solidify one's place in the broader campus community and can decrease one's sense of curricular and personal isolation.
- Inclusive learning environment. Welcoming the diverse backgrounds and experiences of learners will increase the groups' collective learning resulting in successful learning communities. Activities should involve participants to reach out and connect with others from different backgrounds from their own whenever possible.

According to CIRTL (2013), the goals of successful learning communities are to:

- develop attitudes and understanding for engaging with all human differences
- acquire tools and skills to help build inclusive working, teaching, and living environments
- effectively interact and communicate across all human differences
- learn and practice ways of engaging with conflict
- build inclusive and equitable relationships across campus and the greater community

When a true community of learners is developed, educators and students find themselves in a positive culture of learning. A community of learners exists when a group of people share values and beliefs while also being actively engaged in learning not only from one another but also student from teacher and teacher from student. In doing this, a learning-centered environment is created in which students as well as educators are constructing knowledge together. Learning communities are designed around mutual respect in a cohesive environment and allow students to connect through sharing resources and points of view in a cooperative and supportive environment.

Creating a positive learning community has many benefits. It supports diverse students' capabilities and enables all members the opportunity to participate at their level of expertise and comfort in a safe environment to make mistakes and ask questions. Providing this support motivates students and results in more willingness to persist when they are challenged or confused. "Environments that foster beliefs of competence through effort can create a secure sense of belonging; one's interest, commitment, and progress matter more than one's perceived ability" (Inzlicht, Good, Levin, & van Laar, 2006). Thus, greater engagement and academic achievement occur because a safe community in which students and teachers are allies has been created.

Whether school systems are interested in building learning communities within specific classrooms or school-wide, it is suggested that these three things exist:

- Encourage, expect, and require authentic collegiality among the adults in the system
- Model, encourage, and expect student participation and active engagement

- Set high expectations for all students while providing appropriate social and academic supports

In order to ensure that all students participate in high-interest educational activities, teachers must take the time to plan carefully to incorporate personally relevant material. When a teacher fails to recognize and address students' unique backgrounds, the skills needed to be a global citizen in their adult years will be nonexistent. This is why the academic experiences and parental perceptions are so crucial in students' attitudes toward education. In creating enthusiastic, lifelong learners, teachers need to show students that what they learn in school will prepare them with skills needed to have fulfilling, productive lives.

Students' performance is highly affected by teachers' expectations. Realistic and high expectations are not only held high for the teachers themselves, but also for all students. This expectation is reflected in the classroom climate created and the positive perception of their students' ability to succeed. Classrooms where students are expected to be hardworking, interested, and successful produce students who are. This has been supported by the research which finds that students who feel they have supportive, caring teachers are more motivated to engage in academic work than students with unsupportive, uncaring teachers (McCombs, 2001).

"Anchored in respect, honor, integrity and a deep belief in the possibility of transcendence, culturally responsive caring places teachers in an ethical, emotional and academic partnership with diverse students" (Gay, 2000, p. 52). Based on holistic or integrated learning, teachers build community among diverse learners in a culturally responsive model in order for students to better understand the pros and cons of moral and political elements. This results in students being obligated to take social action to promote freedom, equity, and justice for everyone.

Chapter Five

Reshaping the Curriculum

> *"In our multicultural society, culturally responsive teaching reflects democracy at its highest level. It means doing whatever it takes to ensure that every child is achieving and ever moving toward realizing his or her potential."*
>
> —Joyce Taylor-Gibson

One of the greatest challenges educators face in today's classrooms is that of student diversity. "Students come to class with different levels of competence and academic preparation, different degrees of motivation to succeed in school work, different social skills and levels of maturity" (Hawley, 2007). In addition to these differences, are the differences in student race, culture, socioeconomic status, and belief systems. Even with the wealth of research and statistical evidence, education continues to focus on white, middle-class students. In today's schools students of color are taught a test-driven Eurocentric curriculum that does not connect with their historical and sociocultural experiences.

While some educators believe there is a need for a national curriculum and standards, the differences students bring require instructional and curricular differentiation in order to address the varying needs of all. Not only do academic needs require attention, school reform must also implement programs that address the diverse social and emotional needs of today's students. By including guidance counseling, character education, and providing social worker services, schools are better prepared to assist culturally diverse students in achieving educational success.

The most important outcome of the schooling process is what curriculum describes in writing. Because curriculum is based on standards, it follows that curriculum and standards are linked as curriculum specifies how the standard is met. In today's schools, high-stakes testing has a strong impact on curriculum design. This document is a plan that focuses and guides classroom instruction and assessment and resides in the district files as what is important to teach.

Now that a little light has been shed on what curriculum is, let's look at what it is not. Curriculum does not tell the district's teachers how the standards should be met. In order for schools to bring all students to high standards, districts need to examine their stance on curriculum. Districts need to decide exactly what purpose curriculum plays in helping teachers understand and deliver to students what is important for students to learn.

Educators need to decide the direction in which the course of events will flow. They must ask the golden question, "Where and how do we want students to come out?" Many schools design their curriculum based on the National Curriculum and Standards. Below are some of the pros and cons of such an approach taken from Sweetland (2005).

Pros and Cons of a National Curriculum and Standards
National Curriculum (curriculum definition below)

Pros

- Practical—provides a framework from which teachers can work
- Agreement on broad common principles
- Provides for equality of educational opportunity access to knowledge for all students
- Goal is to ensure vocational and economic success for individual and nation
- Easier to transfer between schools
- Less expensive
- Fill political agendas
- Less teacher education with the teacher as a facilitator
- Curriculum focus on basic skills
- Teach to the test
- Easy to assess

Cons

- Not every school is the same
- Student achievement based solely on external tests
- Focus on product instead of process (lack of critical thinking, problem solving)
- Focus on societal needs as compared to individual
- Less professional freedom and judgment, teacher autonomy, teacher as a technocrat
- More competitive on an individual basis—no collaborative effort

- Values are excluded subject orientation
- Doesn't realize the complexity of curriculum development
- Lose teachable moments
- Lack of democratic value without a democratic process
- Lose student-teacher interaction
- Lack of creativity
- Lose student autonomy
- Imposed ideologies
- Imposed religion
- False sense of democracy
- Lose community support
- Narrow scope

Standards

Pro

- Need to know what needs to be taught—guidelines

Con

- Standards are written and enforced by noneducators

Balanced Curriculum

Pros

- Looks at the whole curriculum—research-based—individualized
- Teachers have to know curriculum development, subject matter, students . . .

Cons

- Takes time to develop, constantly changing

- More expensive
- Difficult to assess

Curriculum Includes

- Connection to standards, community needs, and student needs
- Teacher empowerment
- Principled procedures
- Flexibility and ability to change
- Timeline
- Whole curriculum descriptions
- Hidden curriculum imbedded
- Objectives or outcomes
- Assessment (formative, summative, diagnosis, generative)
- Evaluation
- Ways to satisfy accountability

Source: Sweetland (2005)

If curriculum is to reflect the goals of a school and the needs of its students, it makes sense for teachers to be highly involved in the development.

To better help students uphold and emphasize their abilities, curriculum content must be viewed as a valuable tool. Dewey (1887) stated that "curriculum must be 'psychological' if it is to be relevant, interesting and effective to student learning." Culturally relevant curriculum requires that the delivery of content be made in meaningful ways to affect the students for whom it is intended. One method is to validate personal experiences and cultural heritages or teach culturally diverse students new content in ways that make comprehension easier.

THE IMPORTANCE OF TEXTBOOKS AS CURRICULUM CONTENT

One of the challenges in developing curriculum is the reality that every school is different. The first step in reshaping the curriculum is to commit to knowing the students you teach and to deepen their understanding by exploring less material but in more depth. Educators must recognize that curriculum not only includes content knowledge, but also the student, community, and teacher's interactions, as well as the understanding and everything that demonstrates it. Using this as a lens for clarity, the daily decisions made not only affect the school's organization and culture, but are the defining factor in curriculum along with the choice of what books to use. Research in the 1980s and 1990s revealed that textbooks were the basis of 70 to 95 percent of all classroom instruction (Tyson-Bernstein & Woodward, 1991; Wade, 1993). Today, even though the rate has lowered somewhat because of the development and implementation of computer-based technologies and multimedia instructional resources, the most prominent teaching tool is still the textbook.

Textbooks are often the default when looking for a foolproof means of guaranteeing successful teaching and learning. This viewpoint is so strongly embedded into the minds of students that courses being offered without a required text are suspicious and often have few registrants. The majority of textbooks used in today's schools are dominated by the European Americans and therefore reflect their status, culture, and contributions.

Today, ethnic stereotypes, cultural exclusions, and racist illustrations have, for the most part, been eliminated from textbooks (Byrne, 2001), but the overall quality continues to be inadequate. Too little attention is given to different cultures interacting within their community and with those from other ethnic groups especially in the interactions that involve race, racism, other forms of oppression, and conflict or experiences that are different than the mainstream norms of society.

One key argument against the use of textbooks is that classroom teachers do not use them effectively. Many try to get through the text within one year from cover to cover which is insane because no student can possibly absorb that amount of information in a year. This approach is torture for all involved, not teaching.

The coverage in textbooks of cultural diversity is inadequate and could be avoided if they included accurate wide-ranged content about the histories, cultures, and experiences of different ethnic groups. To address this deficiency, teachers need to supplement with other resources. Along those same lines, it is unlikely that any one author, book, or reference would ever be capable of providing a complete portfolio of all ethnic groups, their cultures, contributions, and experiences. This results in the need for teachers to use a combination of resources to do a better job of addressing these areas. Because this requires research and prep time, many overworked educators allow the textbook to drive instruction instead of developing a more demanding curriculum.

I want to be clear on this point. I am not suggesting that textbooks should not be used. There are many excellent textbooks available on the education market, but there is no perfect text that will meet all the needs that arise in your classroom. The most effective content is often created using an eclectic approach in which the most useful ideas, strategies, and activities are pulled from a variety of resources. In order to make the best decision, educators need to know where their students' needs are, their instructional objectives, and how their personal teaching preferences affect them.

THE TYPES OF CURRICULUM

Gay (1995) identifies that three types of curricula are routinely present in today's classrooms. Each offers different opportunities for teaching cultural diversity.

1. Formal Plans: Policy and governing bodies of the education system. Adopted textbooks and other guidelines such as core standards anchor these plans with national commission, state department of education, and school district policy.

    The strengths and weaknesses of this type of curriculum are well-known by the culturally responsive teacher and this results in supplements and changes being made to correct it. The three main focus points are quantity, accuracy, and complexity in which the culturally responsive teacher implements multiple perspectives in instruction that deal with controversy, while studying a wide range of ethnic individuals and groups within race, class, ethnicity, and gender.
2. Symbolic Curriculum: When educators use the classroom and school walls to assist in the visualization and presentation of various cultural facts and beliefs. Examples of artifacts that can be used are images, icons, awards, and celebrations.

    The use of symbols is a powerful source of persuasion. Culturally responsive teachers use it as an instrument to convey important facts, values, and actions about ethnic and cultural diversity. A good guideline is to use images that represent a wide variety of age, gender, time, and place as well as social class and positional diversity across ethnic groups.

3. Societal Curriculum: Cortés (2000) defines this as "knowledge, ideas and impressions about ethnic groups that are portrayed in the mass media." The most common examples of this are television, newspapers, magazines, movies, and the Internet in which more than factual information or idle entertainment is included. Educators need to be cautious however as much of this information is prejudicial and inaccurate.

Analyzing how ethnic groups and experiences are presented in the media is a key focus for the culturally responsive teacher. Disseminating information through the societal curriculum should be done in order to teach students to be discerning consumers and resisters to ethnic information.

Culturally responsive education students acquire self-identity in the curriculum which often results in an increase in self-esteem and the desire to learn. Societal issues can also be confronted in an open forum for students and educators. This method undermines biases in both the classroom and the curriculum while also delivering a richer, more complex and effective experience for all stakeholders.

When curriculum is culturally responsive it capitalizes on students' cultural backgrounds rather than attempting to override or negate them. It is:

- Integrated and interdisciplinary
- It does not rely on one-time activities, "add on" units, or "sprinkling" the traditional curriculum with a few minority individuals (Hilliard, 1992)
- Develops critical thinking skills

- Often incorporates strategies that utilize cooperative learning and whole language instruction, includes self-esteem building, and recognizes multiple intelligences and diverse learning styles (Association for the Advancement of Health Education, 1994)

While the formal distinctions in general seem important, the terms are perhaps a bit confusing and the classifications are not often useful to curriculum workers. The following concepts may be easier to understand and contain slightly different implications. They are: the **recommended curriculum**, the **written curriculum**, the **supported curriculum**, the **taught curriculum**, the **tested curriculum**, and the **learned curriculum**. The *written,* the *supported,* the *taught,* and the *tested* curricula are considered components of the **intentional curriculum**. When referring to the intentional curriculum, it is the set of learning that the school system consciously intends. The hidden curriculum is almost the total opposite as it is prominently not a product of conscious intent.

When individual scholars, professional associations, and reform commissions recommend a curriculum that encompasses the requirements of the policy-making groups like federal and state government, it is referred to as the recommended curriculum. This curriculum stresses the skills and concepts that should be emphasized based on the perceptions and value system of the sources.

The purpose of written curriculum is mainly to ensure that educational goals of the system are being accomplished which is a controlled curriculum. It is much more specific and comprehensive than curriculum that is recommended in that it supports the general goals to be accomplished, objectives to be mastered, and the sequence of content to be studied along with activities to be used.

The curriculum that is shaped by the resources allocated to support and deliver it is known as the supported curriculum. There are four types of criteria that are important here:

1. Time allocated to a given subject at each grade level of schooling
2. Time allocated by the classroom teacher to address the overall subject matter
3. Personnel availability as reflected by the school/district budget
4. Textbooks and other learning materials provided by the school system

How much conformity exists between the written curriculum and the taught curriculum varies. It seems that there are two extremes to this conformity with every combination in between. There are those school systems claiming a high degree of conformity between written and taught curriculum through the use of curriculum-aligned projects. Then there are others that exercise a curricular anarchy in which each teacher develops their own curriculum with diverse activities being implemented throughout the school.

The tested curriculum comes in many forms including teacher-made classroom tests, in-district developed tests, curriculum reference tests, and standardized tests. The question arises as to what extent these tests are related to the taught curriculum. Answers to this question vary greatly. Tests have evolved from rote memorization of objective information and multiple choice items that truly assess a student's guessing ability to higher-order critical thinking approaches that implement real-world situations.

The term learned curriculum for this book's purpose applies to all the changes in values, perceptions, and behaviors that occur related to school experiences. This includes what the student understands, learns, and retains from the intentional curriculum as well as from the hidden curriculum.

You may be wondering exactly what students learn and retain from intentional curriculum. This is really an unanswerable question because it is hard for a teacher to know what works and what does not when it comes to school mission and academic goals. This starts with students' sensitivity to the accountability system in place in the classroom and expresses concern for what exactly they are held accountable.

For students to have success in an accountability-oriented classroom, they must invent strategies for managing uncertainty and reducing risk. It is human nature to restrict output to others and give vague and limited answers until trust is formed and it is known to be safe to make mistakes. Once this is established, students will increase the certainty of teachers' instructions by asking them for more examples or clarity of expectations. Students will often try to pressure teachers into simplifying curriculum by resisting critical thinking or problem solving and discovery. Although No Child Left Behind was implemented to address many of these issues through accountability and testing, "it is not as effective as the student learning culture for promoting achievement" (Firestone, 2009).

CURRICULUM QUALITY

The million dollar question all educators ask is "What constitutes a high-quality curriculum?" This cannot be answered easily since the definition of high quality is based on personal value. Where one school system believes a narrowly focused curriculum dealing with the basics is the quality they desire, another may believe a comprehensive, broad curriculum that includes life-related issues is the best approach. Finding one curriculum which all parties agree is high quality is a next-to-impossible task, however, there are several research-based guidelines for developing a high-quality curriculum:

1. The curriculum should be structured so students and teachers are allowed to study important topics and skills in greater depth. In other words, go deeper instead of broader. Several studies have found that by focusing in-depth on fewer skills and concepts, greater understanding and retention is achieved while also supporting efforts to teach problem solving and critical thinking. (See, for example, Knapp & Associates, 1991.)
2. The structure of curriculum should require students to use various learning strategies in order to solve problems. Critical-thinking skills need to be embedded in the units taught so they are better learned and retained. (For more detailed discussion of this issue, see the volume edited by Grennon Brooks & Brooks, 1993.)
3. The curriculum's structure and delivery should entail students acquiring both the essential skills and knowledge of the subjects. An ongoing argument has occurred between educators as to the power of content versus process in curriculum. Students are only able to solve complex problems when given access to the knowledge they need to solve them. When students call to mind what is needed to solve problems, this is called generative knowledge. An example would be if students learn the capital of Michigan and keep that in their memory, it is inert knowledge. If they learn where the capital

is and use that knowledge to write to the governor, then the knowledge becomes generative.
4. The curriculum should be structured in order to respond to students' individual differences. There are three types of responsiveness recommended:

    a. modes of representation need to be varied based on the way people display or transfer knowledge.
    b. a gradual release model should be used so teachers provide a high degree of structure by using cues, suggestions, and explanations at the beginning of the year and as the year progresses, students are solving problems on their own.
    c. multiple intelligences of students need to be recognized and addressed. Often, curriculum only addresses the verbal and mathematical but high-quality curriculum needs to address all levels.

5. Curriculum should be organized so that it provides multiyear sequential studies, not "stand-alone" courses. This approach results in greater pay-off than single courses that are not a part of an overall study program (McDonnell, 1989).
6. There should be a link between academic and applied knowledge throughout the curriculum. It should emphasize both the academic and the practical and not just appear in tech prep courses (Johnson, 1989).
7. Curriculum should be integrated which results in better achievement and improved attitudes toward schooling. The goal of integration, however, should not come at the expense of other goals. Leaders and teachers should work together to

decide the type and extent to which integration should happen.
8. The focus should be on a limited number of essential curriculum objectives. The goal is the depth of the concept not the breadth (Cotton, 1999).
9. The learned curriculum should have a maintained focus of improving the learning of all students (Schmoker, 1999). The written curriculum is only a means to an end; high-quality learning happens for all students.

CURRICULAR GOALS

Curricular goals consist of the long-term educational outcomes that a school system expects to achieve within the curriculum. There are three critical elements in creating curricular goals. First, goals need to be stated much more generally than objectives. For example: one goal for language arts may be to communicate ideas through writing and speaking whereas an objective may state to write a letter suggesting a community improvement in appropriate business letter format. Another element to remember is that goals are long-term not short-term outcomes. The last element of curriculum goals consists of the outcomes the school system hopes the curriculum will achieve.

For clarification, educational goals are long-term outcomes that are expected through the entire educational process. It is extremely important for educators to make clear distinction between educational goals and curricular goals. According to a survey conducted by Brown (Richards, Brown, & Forde, 2006), educators, parents, and employers felt the following skills were what students should be developing throughout their educational years:

1. Critical thinking
2. Problem-solving strategies and effective decision-making skills
3. Creative thinking process
4. Effective oral and written communication skills
5. Basic reading, mathematical, and writing abilities
6. Knowledge of when and how to use research to solve problems
7. Effective interpersonal skills
8. Technology skills
9. Knowledge of good health and hygiene habits
10. Acceptance and understanding of diverse cultures and ethnicities
11. Knowledge of how to effectively manage money
12. Willingness, strategies, and ability to continue education

An effective instructional practice loses effectiveness if the curriculum isn't strong enough. Conversely, having high academic standards isn't enough if they are not implemented through powerful instructional methods. So where does a school system start?

At the turn of the century, Marzano, Pickering, and Pollock (2001) noted that when developing units of study at any level, it is best to view the process as a series of phases. Based on this principle, Mooney and Mausbach (2008) state that in order for districtwide improvement to happen, teachers must have the time to revise and develop curriculum that is focused on instruction and therefore suggest the following steps for developing curriculum:

1. Establish the foundation setting the tone for the entire planning and developing process.

2. Data analysis: focus on developing a common understanding of the district's needs and use student data to define strengths and weaknesses.
3. Assessments: help curriculum development by establishing local benchmarks that will help teachers identify how well students understand the big ideas outlined in the curriculum standards (Wiggins & McTighe, 1998).
4. Writing: begin to create supporting curriculum documents that teachers can use to implement the curriculum in the classroom, which includes developing a curriculum guide.
5. Resource review: the team reviews and selects resources that align with the standards, grade-level expectations, and assessments the team developed.
6. Pilot process: team plots the data based on implementing materials with students.
7. Board approval: updating and asking the board of education to adapt the new curriculum.
8. Staff development: most critical phase as it needs to be ongoing and collaborative.
9. Implementation: this is where the rubber meets the road. The team uses assessments developed to help measure whether the curriculum is meeting the needs.

PRODUCING A HIGH-ACHIEVING LEARNING ENVIRONMENT

Shannon & Bylsma (2004) define the nine characteristics of a High-Performing School as:

1. **A Clear and Shared Focus**: Achieve a shared vision and all understand their role in achieving that vision.

2. **High Standards and Expectations for All Students**: Some students must overcome significant barriers. Teachers and staff believe that all students can learn and meet high standards.
3. **Effective School Leadership**: Effective leaders are proactive and seek help that is needed. They nurture an instructional program and school culture conducive to learning and professional growth.
4. **High Levels of Collaboration and Communication**: Strong teamwork among teachers across all grades and with other staff. Everyone is involved and connected to each other.
5. **Curriculum, Instruction, and Assessments Aligned with State Standards**: Research-based teaching strategies and materials are used. Staff understands the role of classroom and state assessments, what the assessment measures are, and how work is evaluated.
6. **Frequent Monitoring of Learning and Teaching:** A steady cycle of different assessments identifies students who need help. More support and instructional time are provided to students who need help. Teaching is adjusted based on frequent monitoring of student progress.
7. **Focused Professional Development:** Strong emphasis placed on training staff in areas of most need. Feedback from learning and teaching focuses extensive and ongoing professional development. Support is aligned with school/district vision
8. **Supportive Learning Environment:** School has a safe, civil, healthy, and intellectually stimulating learning environment. Students feel respected and connected with staff and are engaged in learning.

9. **High Levels of Family and Community Involvement:** There is a sense that all have a responsibility to educate students, not just the teachers. Families as well as businesses, social service agencies, and community colleges/universities all play a vital role in this effort.

In high-achieving learning environments for all students, the most advanced curriculum and instruction techniques combine to support learning. Teachers need to create an environment that engages students in complex problem solving as they explore ideas and issues by drawing on a student's culture, experiences, and knowledge. Learning activities are challenging and aligned with learning goals while promoting engaged learning based on culture, life experiences, and knowledge of all students. Issues are analyzed by allowing students to discuss, argue, and dissect concepts from various viewpoints which builds understanding from in-depth investigation.

Multicultural content infused throughout the curriculum is another aspect of curriculum that leads to higher expectations. This approach develops cultural sensitivity while also honoring students' home cultures but is a difficult balance to perform without intensifying cultural and language stereotypes. Some suggestions based on research for producing a high-achieving learning environment include reshaping the curriculum by:

1. Focusing on complex, meaningful problems that make sense to students
2. Including basic skills that are embedded in the context of broader, more complex, and more meaningful tasks

3. Making connections to students' experiences outside of school from their own culture which will encourage students to bring their own real-life problems to school to discuss
4. Using resources other than textbooks for study
5. Having students research aspects of a topic within their community
6. Encouraging students to interview members of their community that have knowledge on the topic being studied
7. Providing information on the alternative viewpoint or beliefs on a topic
8. Developing learning activities that reflect students' backgrounds
9. Including cooperative learning strategies
10. Allowing students the choice of working alone or in groups on certain projects
11. Developing integrated units around universal themes

BUILDING BLOCKS OF SUCCESSFUL DIFFERENTIATED INSTRUCTION

When a teacher teaches students the same thing in the same way, usually the result is that some students "get it" and some don't. Klingner et al. (2005) believe that culturally and linguistically diverse students can excel in school when they have access to high quality teachers, programs, and resources that value their culture, language, and heritage. Regardless of the issues or problems a student might face, the right teaching approach can increase what the student will learn. Educators need to adjust the curriculum and instruction to meet students' differences. "Our choice isn't between sending them down the hall or do nothing. We can differentiate in the regular classroom" (Hess, 1999).

The principle behind differentiated instruction tends to lend itself to the culturally responsive pedagogical approach in that it creates opportunities for countless investigations into one lesson or topic at the same time. Students of color can explore a topic through a differentiated teaching approach designed to meet their learning style, while also allowing examination of the values, beliefs, and ideas that shape their experiences.

According to Forsten, Grant, and Hollas (in progress) there are seven "building blocks" to successful differentiated instruction. Within the combination of these elements reflects an approach to teaching and learning that addresses the needs of culturally and linguistically diverse students. These building blocks invite teachers to add elements to each in order for them to be able to do things differently for different children. The seven building blocks are outlined below:

1. **Knowing the Learner:** In order for teachers to teach students well, they need to know the students' learning styles and pace, their multiple intelligences as well as personal qualities such as personality, temperament, and motivation, health, family circumstances, and language preference.
2. **Traits of a Quality Teacher:** Ask any educator and they will tell you all students can learn. High-quality teachers also have the desire and capacity to differentiate curriculum and instruction, understand diversity, are open to change, are risk takers, are well-versed in best practices, and know what works and what doesn't.
3. **Quality Curriculum:** Students need a curriculum that is not only interesting, but relevant to their lives. It also needs to be challenging, thought provoking, and contain a focus on quality, not quantity, meaning depth in learning.

4. **Classroom Learning Environment:** To create the ideal learning environment, teachers must have a balanced student population with priority seating based on student needs. Students need to be at an appropriate grade level and program placement with a reasonable class size, flexible grouping opportunities, and adequate teaching supplies.
5. **Flexible Teaching and Learning Time Resources:** Includes team teaching, block scheduling, tutoring and remediation within school, before- and after-school programs, homework clubs, multiage/looping classrooms.
6. **Instructional Delivery and Best Practices:** There are many elements to this building block including flexible grouping, cooperative learning, learning stations and centers, web quests, tiered assignments, individual contracts, and literature circles to name a few. If teachers are able to recognize that they are some person teaching something to some students somewhere (Irvine, 2003, p. 48), they will be able to view their teaching with a "cultural eye," thus combating the assimilationist perspective that standardizes students and curricula.
7. **Assessment, Evaluation, and Grading:** Includes portfolios, observations, skills checklists, oral and written reports, demonstrations, performances, work samples, models, taped responses, drawings, graphs and posters, quizzes and tests, and standardized tests.

Morey and Kilano (1997) recognize three levels of curriculum transformation with higher-order cultural responsiveness being the final goal.

1. Exclusive (lowest level): Involves traditional mainstream perspectives of diversity. Instructional strategies are comprised mainly of lecture, basic question-and-answer with a teacher-centered instructional approach.
2. Inclusive: Includes retaining the traditional, original structure, but adds diversity content. Instruction remains teacher-centered, however, a variety of methods are used to relate new knowledge including the use of various speakers to add depth.
3. Transformed: Challenges the traditional views and promotes new ways of thinking. Instruction is student-centered and content is related and requires application and examination of one's values.

Effective multicultural curriculum needs to infuse academic success skills and effective learning strategies. Most textbook selections evolve from policies of several large states like California, Texas, and Florida who require publishers to reflect diversity, but do not specify percentages for particular groups. Textbook selection and curriculum development need to be carefully analyzed so that they address higher-order critical thinking skills while integrating real-world cultural beliefs and differences.

Chapter Six

Culturally Responsive Lessons, Lesson Plans, and Assessment

"When you learn something from people or from a culture, you accept it as a gift, and it is your lifelong commitment to preserve it and build on it."

—*Yo-Yo Ma*

Lesson plans are a teacher's road map of what students need to learn, but also how it will be done effectively during a specific class time. The educator needs to identify the learning objectives and then design appropriate learning activities that include methods of obtaining feedback on the student learning. Successful lesson plans should have three key components:

- Objectives for student learning
- Higher-order teaching/learning activities
- Strategies to check student understanding

In order to determine the kinds of teaching and learning activities that will be used in the classroom, teachers must specify concrete objectives for student learning. The activities then define the assessment of how successfully the learning objectives were mastered.

CULTURALLY RESPONSIVE LESSONS

In the culturally responsive classroom, learning experiences typically last twenty to ninety minutes and focus on a small number of objectives. This means classroom teachers must realize that curriculum planning should emphasize metacognitive control of all processes. Similar to skills, these processes often produce some form of product or new understanding. Today's educators recognize the importance of metacognition, but are unfamiliar with its many dimensions.

The following analytical steps produce three types of learning.

1. Divide the learning expected from the students to that which is basic and that which is enrichment. Basic learning is that which is essential for all students. Enrichment learning is that which is knowledge and skills that are interesting and enriching but are not considered essential; they simply are nice to know.
2. Further divide the basic learning into that which requires structure and that which does not require structure.

    a. Structured learning has four characteristics:

    - Sequencing
    - Planning
    - Measurable Outcomes
    - Clearly Delineated Content

b. Nonstructured learning includes all those skills, knowledge, and attitudes that can be mastered without careful sequencing, planning, testing, and delineation.

Improving and enhancing lessons based on current brain research and curriculum design is becoming a critical component in the search for best practices. Marzano and his colleagues (2001) identified nine categories of strategies that have a strong effect on student achievement. They are as follows:

1. Identifying similarities and differences
2. Summarizing and note-taking
3. Reinforcing effort and providing recognition
4. Homework and practice
5. Nonlinguistic representations
6. Cooperative learning
7. Setting objectives and providing feedback
8. Generating and testing hypotheses
9. Questions, cues, and advance organizers

CULTURALLY RESPONSIVE LESSON PLANS

Teachers need to prepare their lesson plans to reflect the cultural diversity within their classroom. The purpose of the lesson plan should be carefully analyzed, keeping in mind what the teacher wants the students to think, know, or do regarding the lesson they teach.

Milkova (2014) suggests six steps that should be used in guiding educators in creating lesson plans. Each step also includes a set of questions designed to prompt reflection and assist in designing high-quality lesson plans.

(1) Outline learning objectives

The first step is to determine what you want students to learn and be able to do at the end of class. To help you specify your objectives for student learning, answer the following questions:

- What is the topic of the lesson?
- What do I want students to learn?
- What do I want them to understand and be able to do at the end of class?
- What do I want them to take away from this particular lesson?

Once you outline the learning objectives for the class meeting, rank them in terms of their importance. This step will prepare you for managing class time and accomplishing the more important learning objectives in case you are pressed for time. Consider the following questions:

- What are the most important concepts, ideas, or skills I want students to be able to grasp and apply?
- Why are they important?
- If I ran out of time, which ones could not be omitted?
- And conversely, which ones could I skip if pressed for time?

(2) Develop the introduction

Now that you have your learning objectives in order of their importance, design the specific activities you will use to get students to understand and apply what they have learned. Because you will have a diverse body of students with different academic and personal experiences, they may already be familiar with the topic. That is why you might start with a question or activity to gauge students' knowledge of the subject or possibly their preconceived notions about it. For example, you can take a simple poll: "How many of you have heard of X? Raise your hand if you have." You can also gather background information from your students prior to class by sending students an electronic survey or asking them to write comments on index cards. This additional information can help shape your introduction, learning activities, etc. When you have an idea of the students' familiarity with the topic, you will also have a sense of what to focus on.

Develop a creative introduction to the topic to stimulate interest and encourage thinking. You can use a variety of approaches to engage students (for example, personal anecdote, historical event, thought-provoking dilemma, real-world example, short video clip, practical application, probing question, etc.). Consider the following questions when planning your introduction:

- How will I check whether students know anything about the topic or have any preconceived notions about it?

- What are some commonly held ideas (or possibly misconceptions) about this topic that students might be familiar with or might espouse?
- What will I do to introduce the topic?

(3) Plan the specific learning activities (the main body of the lesson)

Prepare several different ways of explaining the material (real-life examples, analogies, visuals, etc.) to catch the attention of more students and appeal to different learning styles. As you plan your examples and activities, estimate how much time you will spend on each. Build in time for extended explanation or discussion, but also be prepared to move on quickly to different applications or problems, and to identify strategies that check for understanding. These questions would help you design the learning activities you will use:

- What will I do to explain the topic?
- What will I do to illustrate the topic in a different way?
- How can I engage students in the topic?
- What are some relevant real-life examples, analogies, or situations that can help students understand the topic?
- What will students need to do to help them understand the topic better?

(4) Plan to check for understanding

Now that you have explained the topic and illustrated it with different examples, you need to check for student understanding—how will you know that students are learning? Think about specific questions you can ask students in order to check for understanding, write them down, and then paraphrase them so that you are prepared to ask the questions in different ways. Try to predict the answers your questions will generate. Decide on whether you want students to respond orally or in writing. You can look at Strategies to Extend Student Thinking, http://www.crlt.umich.edu/gsis/P4_4.php, to help you generate some ideas and you can also ask yourself these questions:

- What questions will I ask students to check for understanding?
- What will I have students do to demonstrate that they are following?
- Going back to my list of learning objectives, what activity can I have students do to check whether each of those has been accomplished?

An important strategy that will also help you with time management is to anticipate students' questions. When planning your lesson, decide what kinds of questions will be productive for discussion and what questions might sidetrack the class. Think about and decide on the balance between covering content (accomplishing your learning objectives) and ensuring that students understand.

(5) Develop a conclusion and a preview

Go over the material covered in class by summarizing the main points of the lesson. You can do this in a number of ways: you can state the main points yourself ("Today we talked about . . ."), you can ask a student to help you summarize them, or you can even ask all students to write down on a piece of paper what they think were the main points of the lesson. You can review the students' answers to gauge their understanding of the topic and then explain anything unclear in the following class. Conclude the lesson not only by summarizing the main points, but also by previewing the next lesson. How does the topic relate to the one that's coming? This preview will spur students' interest and help them connect the different ideas within a larger context.

(6) Create a realistic timeline

GSIs know how easy it is to run out of time and not cover all of the many points they had planned to cover. A list of ten learning objectives is not realistic, so narrow down your list to the two or three key concepts, ideas, or skills you want students to learn. Instructors also agree that they often need to adjust their lesson plan during class depending on what the students need. Your list of prioritized learning objectives will help you make decisions on the spot and adjust your lesson plan as needed. Having additional examples or alternative activities will also allow you to be flexible. A realistic timeline will reflect your flexibility and readiness to adapt to the specific classroom environment. Here are some strategies for creating a realistic timeline:

- Estimate how much time each of the activities will take, then plan some extra time for each
- When you prepare your lesson plan, next to each activity indicate how much time you expect it will take
- Plan a few minutes at the end of class to answer any remaining questions and to sum up key points
- Plan an extra activity or discussion question in case you have time left
- Be flexible—be ready to adjust your lesson plan to students' needs and focus on what seems to be more productive rather than sticking to your original plan

So what does a lesson plan look like? It really depends on your teaching style and organizational personality. A great resource for a culturally responsive lesson plan outline/guidelines is: http://notebook.lausd.net/pls/ptl/docs/PAGE/CA_LAUSD/LAUSDNET/ABOUT_US/INITIATIVES/AEMP/CAG_HOME/CRRE_CLEARINGHOUSE/CRRE_CLASS_RESOURCES/AEMP_CRITERIA%20FOR%20LESSON.PDF. Below are a couple of lesson plan outlines for specific grade levels and subjects taken from the *Culturally Responsive Classroom Management and Motivation Handbook* (Muniz, 2008).

Chapter 6

FAMILY QUILTS

Grades: K–2

Skills:

Students will identify shapes, colors, and patterns.

Materials:

- Pictures of quilts
- Pattern blocks
- 1 sheet of white paper
- 1 sheet of construction paper

Instructions:

Teacher will introduce the history of quilts and the use of shapes and family traditions in the construction of the quilts. The class will discuss the use of quilts in various cultures. Teacher will show students various examples of quilts and question students about the use of geometry/shapes and family traditions in quilts.

Students will construct a square for a class quilt using pattern blocks and knowledge from their culture. Provide students with pattern blocks and one sheet of white paper to be folded in four sections.

Allow students to discuss their ideas about their contributions to the quilt. Students will then use various shapes to draw a representation of their family in the first section. Students will share and discuss with the class their quilt square and the use of their culture and shapes in the design. Students will copy their design on the three other squares and cut out the four sections. Instruct students to keep one square for themselves and place the three others face down. Students will walk around the room and take three different squares from their classmates. They will then take their four squares to paste them onto a piece of construction paper, spacing them out to represent a quilt. They can draw threads between the pictures to represent stitching on a quilt. Students will share and discuss with the group their newly constructed quilts. The class will close the lesson by discussing the variations of shapes and geometric patterns used throughout the quilts (EDSITEment, 2002).

MEANINGFUL OBJECTS

Grades: 2–5

Skills:

Students will learn strategies for personal and creative writing. Students will also understand the connection between visual and textual representations.

Materials:

Personally meaningful object, various paper types

Instructions:

Students will bring a personally meaningful object from home. The object can be anything the student feels is representative of their culture. Students will write a poem, essay, or a short description of their object. Symbols, metaphors, or creative language can also be used to describe the object. The teacher will model the steps of the activity, sharing his or her meaningful object and descriptions. Students will share and discuss their object and written description. The objects and their descriptions will then be displayed for students to participate in a gallery walk.

PERSONAL TIMELINE

Grades: 3–4

Skills:

Students will gain knowledge of cultures and family backgrounds through chronological autobiographies.

Materials:

Roll of paper, crayons, markers, colored pencils, etc.

Instructions:

Students will create a personal timeline using a roll of paper. Students will chronologically record significant events on the line with pictures to depict the events. The teacher will then model a biographical timeline using personal events and information. Students will gather information from their families and photographs. Students will begin the timeline with their birth and continue by highlighting important events throughout their life. The dates and descriptions of particular events will be written on the timeline. Photographs, magazines, or illustrations can be used to depict the events. The timelines will then be posted around the classroom for a gallery walk. Students will then share, compare, and discuss their life events with the class.

There are many resources that include lesson plan samples for the culturally responsive classroom. Resources for culturally responsive lesson plan ideas:

1. New Horizons for Learning. A Culturally Responsive Lesson for African American Students: http://www.newhorizons.org/strategies/multicultural/hanley2.htm

2. Teaching Diverse Learners. Culturally Responsive Teaching: http://www.lab.brown.edu/tdl/tl-strategies/crt-research.shtml
3. Differentiated Science and History: http://www.treecenter.org/udl/lessonplans.htm
4. Differentiated Math Lesson, Gr. 6–8: http://www.exemplars.com/math_6-8/math_sample_6-8.html
5. Alternative Ideas for Book Reports, Gr. K–3: http://www.tst1160-35.k12.fsu.edu/elbookreports.html
6. Literature; The Cay. Gr. 5–6: http://tst1160-35.k12.fsu.edu/mid-litcay.html
7. Social Studies; Presidents, Gr. 4: http://tst1160-35.k12.fsu.edu/elsspres.html

CULTURALLY RESPONSIVE ASSESSMENT

Not only is it important to understand the reasons for differentiating assessments but also to have the resources that show ways in which to differentiate. Differentiated assessment allows teachers to know their students are learning what is being taught and allows students to show what they know in a variety of ways.

This is the point in the book you are probably asking yourself "What do we mean by Culturally Responsive Assessment?" There are a variety of assessment methods available for the diverse learner. Teachers should select formal and informal formats that focus on uncovering what students already know and understand in order to capitalize on students' strengths (Richards, Brown, & Forde, 2006). Teachers must recognize while they interpret student assessment results that norms regarding expected student performance may vary depending on students' cultural backgrounds and experiences. Research shows that educators often ignore this variation or view differences as examples of deviance in need of correction (Klingner et al., 2005).

With today's high stakes and accountability, tests play an integral role in decisions about student placement. Unfortunately, too many culturally different students are not scoring well when evaluated on standard assessments which is why it is so important that teachers create and use tests and assessments that are culturally responsive (Whiting & Ford, 2006).

Ford (2010) also states that assessment should be guided, in part, by the following queries:

- Are the measures valid and reliable for the specific culturally different students and group?
- How can educators decrease bias in the measures (for example, tests, checklists, forms, etc.) that they use or must adopt for evaluation and gifted education decisions?
- Relative to the notion of differentiation, have all students had opportunities to be evaluated in ways that have opportunities to show their learning via speeches, presentations, skits, research, and other modalities?

According to The Educational Testing Service (2009) there are three major elements to the culturally responsive assessment:

- **Validity**: The assessment tests the learning objective—and nothing else
- **Equity**: All students have equal opportunity to master learning objectives, regardless of cultural background, economic status, or language
- **Plurality**: Students should be able to function and demonstrate mastery in multiple contexts

Based on Bloom's Taxonomy (2001), teachers can differentiate assessment based on the levels of cognitive domains of learning. The six levels are as follows:

1. **Remembering**: Retrieving, recognizing, and recalling relevant knowledge from long-term memory.
2. **Understanding**: Constructing meaning from oral, written, and graphic messages through interpreting, exemplifying, classifying, summarizing, inferring, comparing, and explaining.
3. **Applying**: Carrying out or using a procedure through executing or implementing.
4. **Analyzing**: Breaking material into constituent parts, determining how the parts relate to one another and to an overall structure or purpose through differentiating, organizing, and attributing.
5. **Evaluating**: Making judgments based on criteria and standards through checking and critiquing.
6. **Creating**: Putting elements together to form a coherent or functional whole; reorganizing elements into a new pattern or structure through generating, planning, or producing.

Based on Bloom's philosophy, the teacher needs to investigate how students learn best and then develop matching assessment strategies. Some examples:

Intelligence	Sample Products
Verbal/Linguistic	Prepare a report, debate, lecture, paper/pencil tests, crosswords, newspaper article
Logical/Mathematical	Apply a formula, solve a problem, use the scientific method, puzzles, experiments, calculations, discover/develop a pattern
Bodily/Kinesthetic	Role-playing, sports games, acting, cooperative learning, dancing, gesturing, mime
Visual/Spatial	Artwork, photographs, posters, PowerPoint, charts, illustrations
Musical/Rhythmic	Sing, tap, create a rap, poem, or jingle
Naturalist	Care for animals/plants, gardening, investigation of nature, experiments, use the scientific method
Interpersonal/People Smart	Teach a part of a lesson, oral presentation, peer tutoring, cooperative group learning, role-play, debate
Intrapersonal/Reflective	Keep a diary, journal, or learning log, independent research, reading, and writing

Bannister (2002) from the Center for Teaching and Learning at the University of North Carolina–Charlotte gives the following examples for various forms of assessment:

- Examples of differentiated Formative Assessment methods:

Teachers check for understanding throughout the lesson and/or unit in order to modify content, process, or presentation if needed.

Suggestions for informal checks for understanding:

a. Hand Signals—thumb up or down, wave hand
b. Index Card Summary—summarize lesson
c. Think and Draw—draw picture(s) of key ideas
d. Web or Concept Map—complete graphic organizer
e. One-Minute Essay—complete a "quickwrite"
f. Oral Questioning—conduct throughout the lesson

- Examples of Assessments producing Written Products and Performances:

Advertisement	Magazine article	Web site	Log Lab report
Biography	Memo Book	Newscast	Play
Brochure	Newspaper article	Collection test	Story
Crossword puzzle	Poem	Editorial	Position paper
Essay	Proposal	Experiment	Script
Research report			

- Examples of Assessments producing Oral Products and Performances:

Audiotape	Conversation	Debate	Discussions

Dramatic reading	Dramatization	Interview	Oral presentation
Oral report	Poetry reading	Puppet show	Radio script
Rap	Skit	Song	Speech
Teach a lesson			

- Examples of Assessments producing Visual Products and Performances:

Advertisement	Graph	Banner	Map
Cartoon	Model	Collage	Painting
Computer graphic	Photograph	Data display	Poster
Design	PowerPoint	Diagram	Website
Questionnaire	Diorama	Scrapbook	Display
Sculpture	Drawing	Slideshow	Filmstrip
Storyboard	Flyer	Videotape	Game

Regardless of the format of the assessment, the educator needs to ask themselves three important questions when creating or designing the assessment itself:

1. Is my assessment an accurate measurement of what I've taught?

    a. Is it aligned with objectives and teaching?
    b. Have I taught my students how to answer this type of question?

2. Is the measured performance a reflection primarily of actual ability or simply one of cultural or linguistic differences?

   a. Do differences in life experiences or family background make portions of the assessment more difficult or inaccessible to diverse students?
   b. Do cultural differences limit students' ability to respond to questions?
   c. Do test materials or methods of responding limit students' ability to respond?

3. Do students display mastery of the material presented? (For example, "But Can They Do Math?")

   a. Do evaluations hold students to high expectations while remaining culturally relevant and flexible?
   b. Do students have multiple opportunities for demonstration of mastery in a variety of culturally diverse and interesting ways?

The main thing to remember when developing lesson plans and assessments is that no matter the subject matter, you must build on your students' life experiences. Holding high academic standards and expectations for all students mixed with enthusiasm encouraging students to reach those standards will undoubtedly result in many of them going beyond.

Conclusion

The effectiveness of culturally responsive teaching on the academic achievement of diverse learners in the K–12 setting is severely lacking in overall empirical research and data. Most research reveals emerging practices and other relevant approaches for educators' consideration. Many of you may be thinking that the majority of these approaches are "just good teaching" examples (Au, 2009). Educators need to remember, however, that there is no generic universality as to what is considered good teaching practice. Teaching and learning in today's classrooms is culturally situated varying across and within cultural and linguistic groups (Gay, 2002).

A continuous and conscious effort needs to be made when implementing these practices so that connections are made to students' cultures, languages, and everyday experiences. "Academic success and cultural identity can and must be simultaneously achieved, not presented as dichotomous choices" (Klingner et al., 2005, p. 23). A rigorous continuum of ongoing professional development must be present in institutions of higher education and school districts to ensure the academic achievement of diverse learners across the United States. Through this support, beginning as well as experienced teachers will not only see the need for but enhance their understanding and implementation of culturally responsive teaching practices.

The most important piece of information is the reminder that cultural competence doesn't occur as a result of a single day of training, or reading a book, or taking a course. Educators become culturally competent over time. The intention of this book is provide a place to start.

Appendix A

The following is one example of a Culturally Responsive Instructional Rubric created by the Clayton State University in Morrow, Georgia. Although it is designed around the state's standards, it is a great example of how teachers can improve their culturally responsive instruction in the classroom.

Appendix A

CSU TEACHER EDUCATION UNIT
DIVERSITY OUTCOMES OBSERVATION RUBRIC

Teacher Candidate: _____
Course#: _____ Date: _____
(Mark one) Practicum: _____ Internship: _____ Other: _____
Lesson Focus: _____ Grade Level: _____

Diagnosis Learning Needs - Candidate uses culturally responsive assessment techniques and technologies to gather and integrate information for all learners.
(Reflects Teacher Education Unit Outcome 1)

Standard	NO/RI	1 - Unsatisfactory	2 - Developing	3 - Target	4 = Exceeds Standard
Diagnoses Learning Needs: Uses Assessments		Candidate rarely draws upon or does not draw upon the results of formal or informal assessments to identify culturally responsive teaching strategies and learning activities (1d).	Candidate inconsistently or ineffectively draws on the results of formal or informal assessments to identify culturally responsive teaching strategies and learning activities (1d).	Candidate consistently and proficiently draws on the results of formal or informal assessments to identify culturally responsive teaching strategies and learning activities (1d).	Candidate consistently and proficiently draws on the results of formal and informal assessments to identify culturally responsive teaching strategies and learning activities (1d).
Diagnoses Learning Needs: Identifies Skills, Concepts and, Vocabulary		Candidate rarely identifies or does not identify culturally relevant skills, concepts, and vocabulary needed for learning activities (1a).	Candidate inconsistently or ineffectively identifies culturally relevant skills, concepts, and vocabulary needed for learning activities (1a).	Candidate consistently and proficiently identifies culturally relevant skills, concepts, or vocabulary needed for learning activities (1a).	Candidate consistently and proficiently identifies culturally relevant skills, concepts, and vocabulary needed for learning activities (1a).

Plans for Student Learning - Candidate plans culturally responsive teaching and culturally responsive curriculum development.
(Reflects Teacher Education Unit Outcome 2)

Standard	NO/RI	1 - Unsatisfactory	2 - Developing	3 - Target	4 = Exceeds Standard
Plans for Student Learning: Plans Integrate Varied Learning Styles		Candidate's lesson plans rarely include or do not include varied learning styles (2b).	Candidate's lesson plans inconsistently or ineffectively include varied learning styles (2b).	Candidate's lesson plans consistently and proficiently include varied learning styles (2b).	Candidate's lesson plans consistently and proficiently go above and beyond expectations in including multiple learning styles (verbal, visual, & active strategies) (2b).
Plans for Student Learning: Plans Integrate Culturally Relevant Interests		Candidate's lesson plans rarely integrate or do not integrate culturally relevant student interests (2e).	Candidate's lesson plans inconsistently or ineffectively integrate culturally relevant student interests (2e).	Candidate's lesson plans consistently and proficiently integrate culturally relevant student interests for most students (2e).	Candidate's lesson plans consistently and proficiently go above and beyond expectations in integrating culturally relevant student interests for all cultures represented (2e).

Appendix A 111

		1 - Unsatisfactory	2 - Developing	3 - Target	4 = Exceeds Standard
Plans for Student Learning: Plans Integrate Multiple Perspectives		Candidate's lesson plans rarely integrate or do not integrate multiple perspectives of content (2e).	Candidate's lesson plans inconsistently or ineffectively integrate multiple perspectives of content (2e).	Candidate's lesson plans consistently and proficiently integrate multiple perspectives of content (2e).	Candidate's lesson plans consistently and proficiently go above and beyond expectations in integrating multiple perspectives of content (2e).
Plans for Student Learning: Plans Integrate Appropriate Inst. Acc		Candidate's lesson plans rarely include or do not include instructional accommodations for individual learning needs (2c).	Candidate's lesson plans inconsistently or ineffectively include instructional accommodations for individual learning needs (2c).	Candidate's lesson plans consistently and proficiently include instructional accommodations for individual learning needs (2c).	Candidate's lesson plans consistently and proficiently go above and beyond expectations in including Instructional accommodations for individual learning needs (i.e., ELL, students with disabilities, etc.) (2c).

Facilitates Student Learning - Candidate facilitates learning that meets the cultural/different learning styles of all learners.
(Reflects Teacher Education Unit Outcome 3)

Standard	NO/RI	1 - Unsatisfactory	2 - Developing	3 - Target	4 = Exceeds Standard
Facilitates Student Learning: Communicates High Expectations		Candidate rarely communicates or does not communicate high standards and expectations throughout the lesson (3b).	Candidate inconsistently or ineffectively communicates high standards and expectations throughout the lesson (3b).	Candidate consistently and proficiently communicates high standards and expectations throughout the lesson (3b).	Candidate consistently and proficiently communicates high standards and expectations throughout the lesson (3b).
Facilitates Student Learning: Uses Varied Pedagogical Techniques		Candidate behavior rarely uses or does not use uses varied pedagogical techniques (3c).	Candidate inconsistently or ineffectively uses varied pedagogical techniques (3c).	Candidate consistently and proficiently uses varied pedagogical techniques (3c).	Candidate consistently and proficiently uses varied pedagogical techniques (individual, pair, or small and large cooperative groups, practice, Socratic dialog, research projects, problem solving, etc.) (3c).
Facilitates Student Learning: Relates Concerns to Content		Candidate rarely relates or does not relate student/community-relevant examples, unexpected situations, and current events to content (3d).	Candidate inconsistently or ineffectively relates student/community-relevant examples, unexpected situations, and current events to content (3d).	Candidate consistently and proficiently relates student/community-relevant examples, unexpected situations, or current events to content (3d).	Candidate consistently and proficiently relates student/community-relevant examples, unexpected situations, and current events to content (3d).
Facilitates Student Learning: Addresses Individual Differences and Needs		Candidate rarely addresses or does not address individual student differences and needs (3b).	Candidate inconsistently or ineffectively addresses individual student differences and needs (3b).	Candidate consistently and proficiently addresses individual student differences and needs (3b).	Candidate consistently and proficiently goes above and beyond expectations in addressing individual student differences and needs (3b).

Demonstrates Appropriate Knowledge - Candidate is knowledgeable of multiculturalism (race, gender, class, ethnicity, special needs, religion) and socio-cultural influences on subject-specific learning. (Reflects Teacher Education Unit Outcome 4)

Appendix A

Standard	NO/RI	1 - Unsatisfactory	2 - Developing	3 - Target	4 = Exceeds Standard
Demonstrates Appropriate Knowledge of Varied Perspectives		Candidate rarely displays or does not display knowledge and acceptance regarding various perspectives/voices in or out of content area (4c).	Candidate inconsistently or ineffectively displays knowledge and acceptance regarding various perspectives/voices in or out of content area (4c).	Candidate consistently and proficiently displays knowledge or acceptance regarding various perspectives/voices in or out of content area (4c).	Candidate consistently and proficiently displays knowledge and acceptance regarding various perspectives/voices in or out of content area (4c).
Demonstrates Appropriate Knowledge of Students' Cultural Backgrounds		Candidate rarely displays or does not display knowledge of cultural diversity in general, and/or students' cultural backgrounds in particular (4c).	Candidate inconsistently or ineffectively displays knowledge of cultural diversity in general, and students' cultural backgrounds in particular (4c).	Candidate consistently and proficiently displays knowledge of cultural diversity in general, and students' cultural backgrounds in particular (4c).	Candidate consistently and proficiently goes above and beyond expectations in displaying knowledge of cultural diversity in general, and students' cultural backgrounds in particular (4c).
Demonstrates Appropriate Knowledge of SocioCultural Influences on Learning		Candidate rarely displays or does not display awareness of sociocultural influences on subject-specific learning (4b,d).	Candidate inconsistently or ineffectively displays awareness of socio-cultural influences on subject-specific learning (4b,d).	Candidate consistently and proficiently displays awareness of socio-cultural influences on subject-specific learning (4b,d).	Candidate consistently and proficiently goes above and beyond expectations in displaying awareness of socio-cultural influences on subject-specific learning (4b,d).

Fosters Student Well-Being – Teacher interacts with diverse students, school, colleagues, parents, and agencies to foster student well-being and learning.
(Reflects Teacher Education Unit Outcome 5)

Standard	NO/RI	1 - Unsatisfactory	2 - Developing	3 - Target	4 = Exceeds Standard
Fosters Student Well-Being: Addresses SocioCultural Factors		Candidate rarely identifies or does not identify sociocultural factors beyond the school that hamper student learning and/or rarely uses or does not use resources within the school and community to mitigate these factors (5a).	Candidate inconsistently or ineffectively identifies sociocultural factors beyond the school that hamper student learning and uses resources within the school and community to mitigate these factors (5a).	Candidate consistently and proficiently identifies sociocultural factors beyond the school that hamper student learning and uses resources within the school and community to mitigate these factors (5a).	Candidate consistently and proficiently goes above and beyond expectations in identifying sociocultural factors beyond the school that hamper student learning and using resources within the school and community to mitigate these factors (5a).
Fosters Student Well-Being: Communicates Effectively With Caregivers		Candidate rarely communicates or does not communicate proactively and/or effectively with caregivers (5b).	Candidate inconsistently or retroactively communicates effectively with caregivers (5b).	Candidate consistently, proficiently, and proactively communicates effectively with caregivers (5b).	Candidate consistently, proficiently, and proactively goes above and beyond expectations in communicating effectively with caregivers (5b).
Fosters Student Well-Being: Demon-		Candidate rarely demonstrates active interest and involvement or does not demonstrate	Candidate inconsistently demonstrates active interest and involvement in	Candidate consistently and proficiently demonstrates active interest	Candidate consistently and proficiently goes above and beyond expectations in demonstrating active interest and involvement in students'

Appendix A

| strates Community Involvement | active interest and involvement in students' community(s) (5c). | students' community(s) (5c). | and involvement in students' community(s) (5c). | community(s) (i.e., attends churches, shops in stores, visits community centers, does service work) (5c) |

Assumes the Role of Professional Teacher – Teacher candidate acts in accordance with the structure, standards and responsibilities of the profession and recognizes the role of the school in supporting a democratic society.
(Reflects Teacher Education Unit Outcome 6)

Standard	NO/RI	1 - Unsatisfactory	2 - Developing	3 - Target	4 = Exceeds Standard
Assumes the Role of Professional Teacher: Demonstrates Caring		Candidate rarely interacts or does not interact with students in a caring and ethical manner (6a).	Candidate inconsistently or ineffectively interacts with students in a caring and ethical manner (6a).	Candidate consistently and proficiently interacts with students in a caring and ethical manner (6a).	Candidate consistently and proficiently goes above and beyond expectations in interacting with students in a caring and ethical manner (6a).
Assumes the Role of Professional Teacher: Demonstrates Cross-Cultural Fairness and Consistency in Classroom Management		Candidate rarely demonstrates or does not demonstrate cross-cultural fairness and consistency in classroom management (6e).	Candidate inconsistently demonstrates cross-cultural fairness and consistency in classroom management (6e).	Candidate consistently and proficiently demonstrates cross-cultural fairness and consistency in classroom management (6e).	Candidate consistently and proficiently goes above and beyond expectations in demonstrating cross-cultural fairness and consistency in classroom management (6e).
Assumes the Role of Professional Teacher: Implements Transformative Multicultural Education Ped.		Candidate fails in his/her/ other's attempt to or does not attempt to implement transformative multicultural education pedagogy.	Candidate inconsistently or ineffectively strives to implement transformative multicultural education pedagogy.	Candidate consistently and proficiently strives to implement transformative multicultural education pedagogy.	Candidate consistently and proficiently implements transformative multicultural education pedagogy (i.e., educational practices that benefit white, male, upper-middle class, or any group to the detriment of other groups are purposely transformed to ensure equity).

- N/O = NOT OBSERVED; *RI =RECOMMEND INTERVENTION (inappropriate candidate behavior worthy of serious concern in the demonstration of this outcome).

Glossary

Cultural Competence: Process of communicating with audiences from diverse geographic, ethnic, racial, cultural, economic, social, and linguistic backgrounds.

Cultural Racism: Value systems that support and allow discriminatory actions against racially and ethnoculturally marginalized communities.

Cultural Responsiveness: Recognition and acknowledgment that society is pluralistic. In addition to the dominant culture, there exist many other cultures based around ethnicity, sexual orientation, geography, religion, gender, and class.

Culture: A body of learned beliefs, traditions, principles, and guides for behavior that are shared among members of a particular group.

Curriculum: An educational term that describes the range of courses from which students choose what subject matters to study, and a sequence of study that includes specific approaches of teaching, learner roles, products, and behaviors, and the assessments used to guide and evaluate learning.

Differentiated Instruction: Teaching philosophy based on the premise that teachers should adapt instruction to student differences.

Racism: A belief that racial differences produce an inherent superiority of a particular race.

References

American Association of Colleges for Teacher Education. (2013). *The Changing Teacher Preparation Profession.* Retrieved from: https://secure.aacte.org/apps/rl/res_get.php?fid=145.

Anstrom, K. (2004). Introduction in Anstrom, K., Glazier, J., Sanchez, P., Sardi, V., Schwallie-Giddis, P., & Tate, P. (Eds). *Preparing all educators for student diversity: Lessons for higher education* (pp. vii–xvii). Washington, DC: Institute for Education Policy Studies, Graduate School of Education and Human Development. The George Washington University.

Ardila-Rey, A. (2008). Language, culture, policy, and standards in teacher preparation. In M. E. Brisk (Ed.) *Language, culture, and community in teacher education.* (pp. 331–351). Mahwah, NJ: Erlbaum.

Argyle, M. (1978). *The psychology of interpersonal behaviour.* London: Penguin.

Association for the Advancement of Health Education. (1994). *Cultural awareness and sensitivity: Guidelines for health educators.* Reston, VA: Author. SP 035064.

Au, K. (2009). Isn't culturally responsive instruction just good teaching? *Social Education, 73*(4), 179–183.

Axtell, R. (1997). *Gestures: The do's and taboos of body language around the world.* New York: John Wiley & Sons.

Banks, J. A. (1999a). *An introduction to multicultural education.* (2nd ed.). Boston, MA: Allyn & Bacon.

———. (1999b). Four approaches to multicultural curriculum reform. In *An introduction to multicultural education.* (2nd ed.). Boston, MA: Allyn & Bacon. *InTime* online. Retrieved from: http://www.intime.uni.edu/multiculture/curriculum/approachs.htm.

Beauboeuf-Lafontant, T. (1999). A movement against and beyond boundaries: "Politically relevant teaching" among African American teachers. *Teachers College Record, 100*(4), 702–723.

Bannister, S. (2002). *Developing objectives and relating them to assessment.* The Center for Teaching and Learning. University of North Carolina–Charlotte.

Bloom, B. S. (Ed.), Engelhart, M. D., Furst, E. J., Hill, W. H., & Krathwohl, D. R. (1956). *Taxonomy of Educational Objectives, Handbook I: The Cognitive Domain.* New York: David McKay Co., Inc.

Blum, R., (2005). A case for school connectedness *Educational Leadership, 62*(7), 16–20.

Borowski, S. (2011). Cultural differences: Bridging the gap. *Insight into Diversity.* Retrieved from: www.insighttodiversity.com/diversity-inclusion/cultural-differences-bridging-the-gap.

Bowman, B., Donovan, M., & Burns, M. (2001). *Eager to learn: Educating our preschoolers.* Committee on Early Childhood Pedagogy, Commission on Behavioral and Social Sciences and Education. National Research Council. National Academy Press, Washington, DC.

Brisk, M. E., & Harrington, M. M. (2000). *Literacy and bilingualism: A handbook for all teachers.* Mahwah, NJ: Lawrence Erlbaum Associates.

Bromley, K. D. (1998). *Language art: Exploring connections.* Needham Heights, MA: Allyn and Bacon.

Byrne, M. M. (2001). Uncovering racial bias in nursing fundamentals textbooks. *Nursing and Health Care Perspectives, 22*(6), 299–303.

Center for the Integration of Research, Teaching, and Learning. (2013). Learning communities. Retrieved from: http://www.cirtl.net/coreideas/learning_communities.

Coalition of Essential Schools. *Student-centered teaching and learning.* Retrieved from: www.essentialschools.org/benchmarks/10.

Cochran-Smith, M. (2004). *Race, diversity, and social justice in teacher education.* New York, NY: Teachers College Press.

Cooper, T. L. (2014). Teacher as facilitator. *Teacher Network.* Retrieved from: www.teachernetwork.org.

Cortés, C. E. (2000). *Our children are watching: How media teach about diversity.* New York: Teachers College Press.

Cotton, K. (1995). *Effective schooling practices: A research synthesis 1995 update.* Portland, OR: Northwest Regional Educational Laboratory.

———. (2000). *The schooling practices that matter most*. Portland, OR: Northwest Regional Educational Laboratory; and Alexandria, VA: Association for Supervision and Curriculum Development.

Damen, L. (1987). *Culture learning: The fifth dimension in the language classroom*. Reading, MA: Addison-Wesley.

Daniels, H. (2002). *Literature circles: Voice and choice in book clubs and reading groups*. Portland, ME: Stenhouse.

Darling-Hammond, L. (1997). *The right to learn: A blueprint for creating schools that work*. San Francisco: Jossey-Bass.

Debenham, L. (2014). Communication—What percent is body language? *Body Language Expert*. Retrieved from: www.bodylanguageexpert.co.uk/communication-what-percentage-body-language.html.

DeSherbinin, J. (2004). White professors can help uproot racism. *The Chronicle of Higher Education*, p. B16.

Dewey, J. (1887). *Psychology*. New York: Harper.

———. (1902). *The child and the curriculum*. Chicago: University of Chicago Press.

Dingus, J. (2003). Making and breaking ethnic masks. In G. Gay (Ed.) *Becoming multicultural educators: Personal journey toward professional agency*. (pp. 91–116). San Francisco, CA: Jossey-Bass.

EDSITEment (2002). *Lesson Plans*. Retrieved from: http://edsitement.neh.gov/lesson-plans.

Educational Testing Service. (2009). *Guidelines for the assessment of English language learners*. Retrieved from: www.ETS.org/s/about/pdf/ell-guidelines.pdf.

Feiman-Nemser, S., & Melnick, S. (1992). Introducing teaching. In S. Feiman-Nemser and H. Featherstone (Eds.) *Exploring teaching: Reinventing an introductory course*. (pp. 1–17). New York, NY: Teachers College Press.

Felder, R. M., & Brent, R. (1996). Navigating the bumpy road to student-centered instruction. *College Teaching, 44*(2), 43–47.

Firestone, W. A. (2009). Accountability nudges districts into changes in culture. *Phi Delta Kappan, 90*(9), 671.

Ford, D. Y. (2010). Culturally responsive classrooms: Affirming culturally different gifted students. *Gifted Child Today, 33*(1), 50–53.

Forsten, C., Grant, J., & Hollas, B. (in progress). A framework for understanding the seven building blocks of differentiated instruction. *Staff Development for Educators*. Retrieved from: www.sde.com.

Fullan, M. (2002). *Change forces with a vengeance*. New York, NY: Falmer Press.

Gay, G. (1995). A multicultural school curriculum. In C. A. Grant & M. Gomez (Eds.), *Making school multicultural: Campus and classroom.* (pp. 37–54). Englewood Cliffs, NJ: Merrill/Prentice Hall.

———. (2000). *Culturally responsive teaching.* New York, NY: Teachers College Press.

———. (2002). Preparing for culturally responsive teaching. *Journal of Teacher Education, 53*(2), 106–116.

Ginott, H. (1995). *Teacher and child.* New York, NY: Collier.

Ginsberg, M. B. (2011). *Transformative professional learning: A system to enhance teacher and student motivation.* Thousand Oaks, CA: Corwin.

Glatthorn, A. A., Boschee, F., Whitehead, B. M., & Boschee, B. F. (2012). *Curriculum leadership: Strategies for development and implementation.* (3rd ed.). Thousand Oaks, CA: Sage Publications, Inc.

Glenn, S. (2014). How to teach in a culturally responsive classroom. *EHow.* Retrieved from: www.ehow.com/how_7869478-teach-culturally-responsive-classroom.html.

Gorski, P., & Covert, B. (2000). Multicultural pavilion: Defining multicultural education. *EdChange.* Retrieved from: http://www.edchange.org/multicultural/define_old.html.

Gray, S. (2012). 5 ways to create a culturally responsive classroom. *National Equity Project.* [Blog]. Retrieved from: http://blog.nationalequityproject.org/2012/08/22/5-ways-to-create-a-culturally-responsive-classroom/.

Grennon Brooks, J., & Brooks, M. G. (1993). *In search of understanding: The case for constructivist classrooms.* Alexandria, VA: ASCD.

Hackett, T. (2003). Teaching them through who they are. In G. Gay (Ed.) *Becoming multicultural educators: Personal journey toward professional agency* (p. 315–340). San Francisco, CA: Jossey-Bass.

Hanley, M. S., & Noblit, G. W. (2009). *Cultural, racial identity and success: A review of literature.* The Heinz Endowment. Retrieved from: http://www.heinz.org/UserFiles/Library/Culture-Report_FINAL.pdf.

Hanly, S. (2014). How to communicate high expectations for elementary students. *Global Post.* Retrieved from: http://everydaylife.globalpost.com/communicate-high-expectations-elementary-students-3650.html.

Hawley, W. D. (Ed.). (2007). *The keys to effective schools: Educational reform as continuous improvement.* (2nd ed.). Thousand Oaks, CA: Corwin Press.

Haynes, P. L. M. (2007). *For cultural competence: A resource manual for developing cultural competence.* Virginia Department of Education.

Herzog, H. W., Jr., Schlottmann, A. M., & Johnson, D. L. (1986). High technology jobs and worker mobility. *Journal of Regional Science, 26*(3), 445–459.

Hess, M. (1999). Teaching in mixed-ability classrooms. Retrieved from: http://www.weac.org/kids/1998-99/march99/differ.htm.

Hilliard, A. G. (1992). The pitfalls and promises of special education practice. *Exceptional Children, 59*(2), 168–172.

Howard, T. C. (2003). Culturally relevant pedagogy; Ingredients for critical teacher reflection. *Theory into Practice, 42*(3), 195–202.

Inzlicht, M., Good, C., Levin, S., & van Laar, C. (2006). How environments can threaten academic performance, self-knowledge, and sense of belonging. In *Stigma and group inequality: Social psychological perspectives* (pp. 129–150). Mahwah, NJ: Lawrence Erlbaum Associates Publishers.

Irvine, J. J. (1990). *Black students and school failure.* Westport, CT; Greenwood Press.

———. (2003). *Educating teachers for a diverse society: Seeing with the cultural eye.* New York, NY: Teachers College Press.

Johnson, J. R. (1989). *Technology: Report of the project 2061 phase i technology panel.* Washington, DC: American Association for the Advancement of Science.

Kea, C. D., & Utley, C. A. (1988). To teach me is to know me. *The Journal of Special Education, 32*(1), p. 44–47.

Klingner, J. K., Artiles, A. J., Kozleski, E., Harry, B., Zion, S., Tate, W., Duran, G. Z., & Riley, D. (2005). Addressing the disproportionate representation of culturally and linguistically diverse students in special education through culturally responsive educational systems. *Education Policy Analysis Archives, 13*(38).

Knapp, M. S., & Associates. (1991). *What is taught, and how, to the children of poverty.* Washington, DC: U.S. Department of Education.

Ladson-Billings, G. (1994). *The dreamkeepers: Successful teachers of African American teachers.* San Francisco, CA: Jossey-Bass.

———. (1997). *The dreamkeepers: Successful teachers of African American children.* San Francisco, CA: Jossey-Bass.

Langdon, H. W. (2009). Providing optimal special education services to Hispanic children and their families. *Communication Disorders Quarterly, 30,* 83–96.

LeBaron, M. (2003). *Bridging cultural conflicts: A new approach for a changing world.* San Francisco: Jossey-Bass.

Lindsey, R., Roberts, L., & Campbell-Jones, F. (2005). *The culturally proficient school. An implementation guide for school leaders.* Thousand Oaks, CA: Corwin Press, A Sage Publications Co.

Little, D. (1999). Developing learner autonomy in the foreign language classroom: A social-interactive view of learning and three fundamental pedagogical principles. *Revista Canaria de Estudios Ingleses, 38*, 77–88.

Lynch, M. (2011). What's culturally responsive pedagogy? *Huffington Post*. Retrieved from: http://www.huffingtonpost.com/matthew-lynch-edd/culturally-responsive-pedagogy_b_1147364.html.

Mahendra, N., Bayles, K. A., Tomoeda, C. K., & Kim, E. S. (2005). Diversity and learner-centered education. *The ASHA Leader*. Retrieved from: http://www.asha.org/publications/leader/2005/051129/f051129c.htm#_ga=1.66753902.1717736670.1428979203.

Marzano, R., Marzano, J., & Pickering, D. (2003). *Classroom management that works: Research-based strategies for every teacher*. Alexandria, VA: Association for Supervision and Curriculum Development (ASCD).

Marzano, R. J., Pickering, D. J., & Pollock, J. E. (2001). *Classroom instruction that works*. Alexandria, VA: ASCD.

McCombs, B. L. (2001). What do we know about learners and learning? The learner-centered framework: Bringing the educational system into balance. *Educational Horizons, 17*, 124–136.

McDonnell, L. M. (1989). *Restructuring American schools: The promise and the pitfalls*. New York: Teachers College, Columbia University Institute on Education and the Economy.

McGee, K. (2008). How cultural differences may affect student performance. *Great Schools*. Retrieved from: http://www.greatschools.org/special-education/support/704-cultural-differences-student-performance.gs.

McHail-Johnson, C., & Costner, K. L. (2004). Seven principles for training a culturally responsive faculty. *Learning Abstracts, 7*(12).

McIntosh, P. (1988). White Privilege and male privilege: A personal account of coming to see correspondences through work in women's studies. (Working Paper no. 189). Wellesley, MA: Wellesley College Center for Research on Women.

McLaughlin, M. W., Langman, J., & Irby, M. (1994). *Urban sanctuaries: Neighborhood organizations in the lives and futures of inner city youth*. San Francisco, CA: Jossey-Bass.

Means, B., & Knapp, M. S. (Eds.). (1991).

Merlino, R. (2007). Addressing cultural diversity in the classroom. Retrieved from: http://www.educationspace360.com.

Milkova, S. (2014). Strategies for effective lesson planning. Center for Research on Learning and Teaching. University of Michigan. Retrieved from: http://www.crlt.umich.edu/gsis/p2_5.

Mooney, N., & Mausbach, A. (2008). *Align the design: A blueprint for school improvement.* Alexandria, VA: ASCD.

Morey, A., & Kilano, M. (1997). *Multicultural course transformation in higher education: A broader truth.* Needham Heights, MA: Allyn and Bacon.

Muniz, A. (2008). *Culturally responsive lessons for students K–5. Culturally responsive classroom management and motivation handbook,* chapter 10. Retrieved from: https://sites.google.com/site/crcmmprojectsite/home.

National Education Association. (2007). *Cultural Abilities Resilience Efforts; Strategies for Closing the Achievement Gaps.* (3rd ed.). Retrieved from: http://www.nea.org/assets/docs/mf_CAREbook0804.pdf.

Nieto, S. (1999). *The light in their eyes: Creating multicultural learning communities.* New York, NY: Teachers College Press.

Noel, J. (2000). *Developing multicultural educators.* New York, NY: Longman.

Noguera, P. (2003). *City schools and the American dream.* New York: Teachers College Press.

Padrón, Y. N., Waxman, H. C., & Rivera, H. H. (2002). *Educating Hispanic students: Effective instructional practices.* (Practitioner Brief #5). Retrieved from: http://www.cal.org/crede/Pubs/PracBrief5.html.

Palardy, G. J., & Rumberger, R. W. (2008). Teacher effectiveness in first grade: The importance of background qualifications, attitudes, and instructional practices for student learning. *Educational Education and Policy Analysis, 30,* 111–140.

Peterson, B. (1994). Teaching for social justice: One teacher's journey. In *Rethinking our classrooms. Teaching for equity and justice.* Milwaukee: Rethinking Schools.

Porter, R. E., & Samovar, L. A. (1991). *Basic principles of intercultural communication. Intercultural communication: A reader* (pp. 5–22). Belmont, CA: Wadsworth.

Quinton, S. (2013). Good teachers embrace their students' cultural backgrounds. *The Atlantic.* Retrieved from: www.theatlantic.com/education/archive/2013/11/Good-teachers-embrace-their-students-cultural-backgrounds/28.

Richards, H. V., Brown, A., & Forde, T. B. (2006). *Addressing diversity in schools: Culturally responsive pedagogy.* Buffalo State College/NCCREST.

Rugsaken, K. (2006). *Body speaks.* Clearinghouse of Academic Advising Resources. Ball State University. Retrieved from: www.nacada.ksu.edu.

Rumberger, R. & Gandara, P. (2004). *Seeking equity in the education of California's English learners.* Teachers College Record, 106, pp. 2031–2055.

Saphier, J., & Gower, R. (1997). *The skillful teacher: Building your teaching skills.* Carlisle, MA: Research for Better Teaching, Inc.

Schmoker, M. (1999). *Results: The key to continuous school improvement.* (2nd ed.). Alexandria, VA: Association for Supervision and Curriculum Development.

Segall, W. E., & Wilson, A. V. (2004). *Introduction to education: Teaching in a diverse society.* (2nd ed.) Lanham, MD: Rowman and Littlefield Publishers.

Shannon, G. S., & Bylsma, P. (2004). *Characteristics of improved school districts: Themes from research.* Olympia, WA: OSPI.

Sheets, R., & Gay, G. (1996). Student perceptions of disciplinary conflict in ethnically diverse classrooms. *NASSP Bulletin, 80*(580), 84–94.

Sweetland, R. (2005*).* *Pros and cons of national curriculum and standards.* Retrieved from: www.homeofbob.com.

Synder, T. (1999). *Digest of education statistics, 1998.* Washington, DC: National Center for Education Statistics. US Department of Education.

Tatum, B. (2003). *Why are all the Black kids sitting together in the cafeteria? A psychologist explains the development of racial identity.* New York: Basic Books.

Thoms, F. (2014). *Teaching that matters: Engaging minds, improving schools.* Lanham, MD: Rowman and Littlefield Publishers.

Tyson-Bernstein, H., & Woodward, A. (1991). Nineteenth century policies for twenty-first century practice: The textbook reform dilemma. In P. G. Altbach, G. P. Kelly, H. G. Petrie, & L. Weis (Eds.), *Textbooks in American society* (pp. 91–104). Albany, NY: State University of New York Press.

Villegas, A., & Lucas, T. (2002). Preparing culturally responsive teachers: Rethinking curriculum. *Journal of Teacher Education, 53*(1). Sage Publication.

Vygotsky, L. S. (1962). *Thought and language.* Cambridge, MA: MIT Press.

Wade, R. (1993). Content analysis of social studies textbooks: A review of ten years of research. *Theory and Research in Social Education, 21*, 232–256.

Weiner, L., (2003). Why is classroom management so vexing to urban teachers? *Theory into Practice, 42*(4), 305–312.

Weinstein, C., Tomlinson-Clarke, S., & Curran, M. (2004). Toward a conception of culturally responsive classroom management. *Journal of Teacher Education, 55*(1), 25–38.

Whiting, G. W., & Ford, D. Y. (2006). Under-representation of diverse students in gifted education: Recommendations for nondiscriminatory assessment (part 2). *Gifted Education Press Quarterly, 20*(3), 6–10.

Wiggins, G., & McTighe, J. (1998). *Understanding by design.* Alexandria, VA: ASCD.

Wilson-Portuondo, M. (2014). Learning within the context of culture. *The Education Alliance* online. Brown University. Retrieved from: www.brown.edu.

Wlodkowski, R. J., & Ginsberg, M. B. (1995). *Diversity and motivation.: Culturally responsive teaching*. San Francisco, CA: Jossey-Bass.

Yedlin, J. (2004). Teacher talk: Enabling ELLs to "grab on" and climb high. Perspectives.

About the Author

Michele M. Wages, PhD, is an instructional specialist serving on Title 1 campuses in the Dallas–Fort Worth area since 1993, including a bilingual campus with an 86 percent Hispanic student enrollment and a free and reduced lunch demographic of 96 percent. During her twenty-six-year career, she has also served as a classroom teacher, reading specialist, language arts facilitator, and has provided staff development training for teachers.

Dr. Wages received her bachelor's degree in social science and elementary education from the University of Michigan in Flint, her master's in educational leadership from Texas Wesleyan University located in Fort Worth, Texas, and her doctorate degree in curriculum and instruction from Capella University in Minneapolis, Minnesota. Her dissertation topic dealt with the effects of two types of bilingual programs on Hispanic student achievement in reading for grades 3–6.

Michele lives in Texas with her two canine companions, Mr. Chips and Bailey, and enjoys her hobbies of gardening, refinishing antique furniture, and old muscle cars. She can be found on many sunny days behind the wheel of her 1967 Ford Mustang.

www.ingramcontent.com/pod-product-compliance
Lightning Source LLC
Chambersburg PA
CBHW030142240426
43672CB00005B/236